Praise for *Disarm Your Limits*

"*Disarm Your Limits* highlights Jessica Cox's triumphs over adversity and gives readers a formula for success in their own lives. Jessica once shared with me that she decided as a young woman to eliminate the words "I can't" from her vocabulary. This book outlines the mechanics of that "can do" spirit and offers great examples of the power of a positive attitude. **A very powerful message for all readers.**"

—STEPHEN R. TAYLOR
PRESIDENT, BOEING BUSINESS JETS

"Jessica Cox demonstrates that you can *Disarm Your Limits* if you think and act "outside the shoe." Jessica herself was born without arms—but ultimately without limits. When I met her, I was impressed by the modest strength of a peerless personality. **Jessica's formula for flight provides incomparable motivation to overcome handicaps, whether you are facing them as an individual, a team, or a corporation.** She is a role model when it comes to turning challenges into opportunities, and we can all learn from her. Each chapter of her unique life, like each chapter of her impressive book, provides great inspiration."

—MICHAEL BUSCHER
FORMER CEO OF OC OERLIKON AND KNORR-BREMSE AG

"A story of inspiration through persistence, faith, and grace."

—PAUL DILCHER
CURTZE FOOD SERVICE

Disarm Your Limits

The Flight Formula to Lift You to Success and Propel You to the Next Horizon

To Donna

Jessica Cox

Disarm Your Limits

The Flight Formula to Lift You to Success
and Propel You to the Next Horizon

Jessica Cox

Rightfooted Publishing
PO Box 35807
Tucson, AZ 85740
For Orders and More Information:
www.jessicacox.com

ISBN
Paperback: 978-0-9863627-0-5
Ebook: 978-0-9863627-1-2

Library of Congress Control Number: 2015933587

Book Project Management: Helen Chang, Author Bridge Media
Editor: Kristine Serio, Author Bridge Media
Book Design: Peri Poloni-Gabriel

First Edition, 2015
Published in the United States of America

Table of Contents

I dedicate this book to you, the reader.

May you use the principles in these pages
to achieve your optimal self and discover
your own formula for flight.
Once you've reached incredible heights,
may you pay it forward to help
someone else do the same.
And may you always remember
that you are not alone, especially when
the skies seem darkest.

May you disarm your limits
and find your wings!

Acknowledgments

DISARM YOUR LIMITS IS a project that has been seven years in the making. I would like to acknowledge the great number of people whose efforts and support made it possible for me to have this beautiful book to share with the world.

First and foremost, thank you to God for putting these amazing people in my life.

Thank you to my husband, Patrick, who gives the best hugs and supports me in all that I do. He has been as proactive as me with this book, working hard to make it the best resource it can be—one that inspires people to be their best selves.

I thank my brother Jason for the many hours of dedication he spent seeing this book through.

My parents have laid a strong foundation for me that has helped me blossom from someone who hated her circumstances to someone who has embraced her challenges as a gift to reach others. I will always be thankful for their support and love.

I am grateful to my "*nanay*," Cora, whose unshakable faith opened my eyes to the greater plan.

My gratitude likewise goes to my sister Jackie, whom I can always count on to be bluntly honest with me.

I would also like to acknowledge all of my other family members and friends who have been there for me throughout this journey.

Finally, I would like to thank Helen Chang, Kristine Serio, and the rest of the Author Bridge Media team. Their work as editors has been truly instrumental in inspiring the world with my story.

Disarm Your Limits

Sky Sprite

Introduction

Everyone has oceans to fly, if they have the heart to do it.

~AMELIA EARHART

Disarmed

PEOPLE OFTEN COME UP to me and say, "How did you go from someone who was upset about not having arms to someone who uses that to inspire others?"

The answer is usually more familiar than they think. Because when you really come down to it, we share a common truth.

In your own way, you were "born without arms," too.

Have you ever felt like you didn't belong? Like you didn't have what it took to reach your goals? Like everything was chaos around you, you didn't have the support you wish you had, and your motivation to keep going was slipping through your fingers?

If any of that sounds familiar, then you know how it feels to be disarmed. Most people think the biggest challenge of not having arms is physical. But the real challenges are social, psychological, and emotional.

The real challenge is the journey to finding acceptance, self-belief, and faith.

Emotional Disability

"Not having arms" may be an emotional disability we all suffer from, in our own way. But here is the good news: you already have everything you need to live the life you've always imagined.

People can't understand how it is possible for me to fly an airplane with my feet. That accomplishment is really the end result of my psychological journey of overcoming obstacles. I overcame fear with courage, shame with acceptance, challenges with innovation—and the list goes on.

I didn't just overcome my disability physically. I also overcame it emotionally and spiritually. You can, too.

You have what it takes to rise above your challenges. You have the ability to turn the obstacles you face around and use them to your advantage. You have the power to look on the bright side of things, and you have the opportunity to use all of that and more to strengthen your faith.

This book will show you how.

The Armless Pilot

Most people know me as "the armless pilot." I have the Guinness World Record for being the first woman to fly an airplane with my feet. And I love flying. But the truth is that becoming a pilot was just one item on my bigger checklist of goals.

I was the first person without arms to get a black belt in the American Taekwondo Association (ATA). In 2014, I became the ATA State Champion for my age division in Forms. I've surfed, skydived, paraglided, and earned my SCUBA certification. I have a Bachelor of Science degree in psychology, and I've spoken to and inspired tens of thousands of people in more than twenty different countries all over the world.

I've been named one of the 100 Most Influential Women in the Filipina Woman's Network. In 2012, I was recognized with the Most Aspirational title from the Inspiration Awards for Women in the United States, followed the next year by the Inspiration International title in the United Kingdom. Plane and Pilot magazine named me as one of their Ten Best Pilots in 2013.

In 2014, I was rated one of the top fifteen Filipino Motivational Speakers by WhenInManila.com. I've spoken for several Fortune 500 companies, including State Farm, Boeing, and international corporations like JPMorgan Chase, Oerlikon, and Mahindra.

I've worked on behalf of people with disabilities at the governmental level, lobbying to ratify the UN Disability Treaty. I'm an advocate for universal disability rights as a Goodwill Ambassador for Handicap International. I've also spoken at the Pentagon in Washington, DC, and the World Economic Forum in Davos, Switzerland.

My story has gone viral on the Internet and has been translated into at least seven different languages. I've heard from people as far away as Namibia, Africa. In 2012, I married my husband Patrick, who means more to me than I can ever express. We fly around the globe together, bringing inspiration to others.

And I've only just begun.

Wing It

This book is your flight manual for success.

In these pages, I will share the story of my journey with you: how I faced down my challenges, and how those obstacles made me into the person I am today. You're on your own journey. At this moment, you are facing challenges that are unique to you, and you probably sense which tool you need most to repair your engine.

Remember that the sky has no street signs, no road dividers, and no double-yellow lines. As you read this book, create your own flight path. If you're facing a fear, skip to the chapter on courage. If you need some extra motivation in the face of a tough challenge, make a beeline for the chapter about persistence.

These concepts and stories are here for you, when you need them. Use them to take flight—your way.

You: The Pilot in Command

The principles in this book are the ingredients that have allowed me to accomplish all that I have done in my life. I've used them to achieve my own success, and I've shown others how to apply them to succeed in their lives, too.

You may be inspired by the stories in these pages. But more importantly, you'll be able to use the principles underneath them to overcome struggles in your own life. You'll recognize blessings in disguise. You'll notice the road signs on your journey to faith, and you'll grow stronger as a result of the difficulties you face. You might even become an inspiration to others.

You will learn how to disarm your limits by turning obstacles into positive opportunities—and that alone can change your world. You will understand the power of hope, and you will experience the promise of emotional inspiration, mental principle, and spiritual strength. You'll recognize that you have everything you need to lift yourself to success and propel yourself to your next horizon.

You are the pilot in command of you. And this book will help you take flight.

"Aviation is proof that,
given the will, we have the capacity
to achieve the impossible."

~EDDIE RICKENBACKER

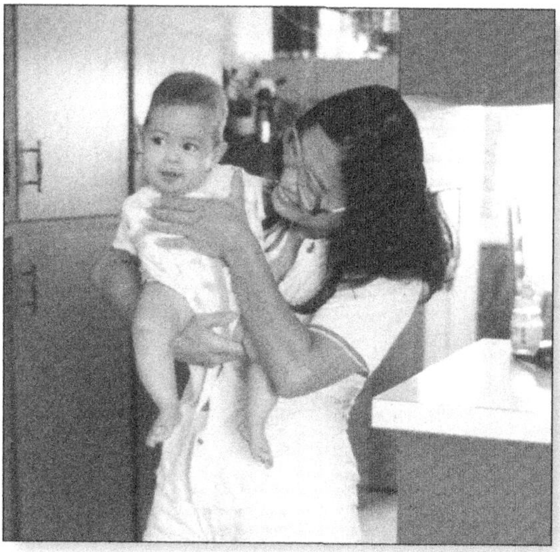

My mom, Inez, holding me as a baby.

1

The Pilot in Command

Your wings already exist. All you have to do is fly.

~ANONYMOUS

Airborne

AS A PILOT, WHENEVER you fly anywhere, you first have to identify "waypoints." A waypoint is a checkpoint programmed into your GPS system that acts as a navigational reference. You stay alert for those checkpoints while you're flying from point A to point B. Every time you pass one, you know that you haven't flown off course. Your waypoints confirm that you're on the right track.

As the pilot in command of you, you use waypoints to guide you to where you want to go, too. But your waypoints aren't navigational references.

They are a set of guiding principles that you can count on to light your way, no matter what.

When it comes to landing lifelong success, I've found that there are a few specific guiding principles that keep you airborne. They are adventure, desire, courage, innovation, balance, persistence, support, authenticity, and faith.

Most of these qualities don't come to us overnight. We develop them as we go through life, celebrating our triumphs and facing our challenges. The path to finding these values isn't always an easy one to walk, whether or not you have arms to help you.

It took me three years to get my pilot's license. But the journey to becoming the pilot in command of me was a runway that spanned decades.

Born without Arms

I was born without arms, completely unexpectedly to both my parents. In the 1980s, ultrasounds were not as advanced as they are today. So they were entirely unprepared.

My birth condition was devastating for them—especially my mother. When I came out through Cesarean section, the doctor was absolutely shocked. Everyone in the delivery room was shocked. For a moment, there was just total silence. My mother couldn't see what had happened, because she was behind the big curtain they put up for surgery. But she knew by their faces that something wasn't right.

"What's wrong?" she demanded.

The doctor looked straight at her and said, "Your baby has no arms."

"One or both?" my mother asked.

"Both," the doctor told her.

And that was it. My mother fell apart, just sobbing and shaking. My dad was next to her, holding her hand. He has always been the rock in our family emotionally, and he's always said that he never once shed a tear over my birth condition. He didn't cry that day; he just started trying to comfort my mom.

I always say that being born without arms robbed me of a very special moment in my life. Because when the doctor proceeded to bring me over to my parents for them to embrace me for the first time, no one reached out to take me. My mother was distraught and my father was struggling to console her. So the doctor turned around again and handed me off to the nurses.

It will always be a void for me that because I didn't have arms, I was denied that first moment with my parents. If I had been born with some kind of internal medical challenge, it would have looked like everything was okay, and they would have been able to embrace me.

Instead, in my very first moments of life, I was already up against the challenge of not being good enough.

"What Happened to Your Baby?"

The genetic tests they ran found no cause for my birth condition. They did body scans to make sure that none of my internal organs were defective, because sometimes that happens. But the rest of me was fine. I just didn't have arms.

My mom is a registered nurse, and she's originally from the Philippines. She's delivered babies there. In developing countries, children born with disabilities often have uncertain fates. They can be shunned, abandoned, or put into institutions. So when she had a disabled child herself, she was just overwhelmed with anxiety and depression, concerned about what kind of future would be in store for me.

But she pulled herself out of it, and she resolved that she was going to do everything in her power to give me a normal childhood.

Sometimes it was hard. We lived in Sierra Vista, Arizona, a small town with about thirty thousand people in it. She'd go to the grocery store with me when I was a baby and a toddler, just to grab a gallon of milk, and everywhere she went she'd be inundated with questions. "Oh, poor baby!" strangers would say. "What happened to your baby?"

My mom always told them, "Don't feel sorry for her. She will be fine."

Toy Tyrant

I always knew that I was different, even when I was very young. I saw my family around me, and I recognized that "Look, I have an older brother there. He has arms. And my younger sister Jackie, she came out with arms. And my parents, they seem to have use of their arms and hands."

I knew that they had something I didn't have. And as a child, I responded to that with anger.

I threw tantrums. I kicked, I screamed, I bit. I was a bratty child, and it was because I was trying to make sense out of the world around me. I just couldn't understand why I was different from everyone else in the world; why people reacted to me differently. A lot of times, that made me so angry that I had to be carried off thrashing and howling by my dad and put in my room.

I was also very selfish with my toys. I felt that even though I couldn't control the outside world and how it reacted to me, I could control my own possessions. So if I was given a toy, I made sure that no one else touched that toy. I wrote my name on it and everything. I was a toy tyrant. And if my brother or sister grabbed one of my toys, I'd attack them. I had an entire swing set to myself in the backyard.

My parents didn't know what to do with me. They wanted to treat me the way they treated everyone else. And my mom had a little bit of a sensitive spot for me, because of my condition. So a lot of the time, I got away with murder.

Keep Up

I learned to move differently than most children.

As a baby, I rolled. Then as a toddler, when other kids learn to crawl, I scooted. I learned to sit up and I just scooted around on my diapers, pushing myself across the floor with my little butt.

Walking was a bigger challenge. Most children grab a hold of furniture when they learn to walk. They get their hands on a coffee table or a couch and they toddle along that way. I didn't have anything to grab on with, so my muscles had to be built up before I could stand. I was about eighteen months old when I first started walking—four or five months behind the average toddler.

I used my feet to do the things that my brother and sister did with their hands. My mom handed dolls or stuffed animals to my feet, and I'd grab hold of them that way. I had a physical therapist who came to teach me some exercises. And I was determined. I explored everything with my toes.

I didn't want to be left behind. Even now, if someone tells me, "Oh, you can't do that, you don't have arms," it gives me more reason to do it. That was true even when I was a toddler. I always felt challenged to keep moving.

Withdrawn

As I grew up through elementary school and junior high, I stopped throwing tantrums and became more withdrawn. For eleven years, I wore prosthetic arms. They were supposed to make my life better, but I hated them. They were clunky and hard to use. Worse, the other kids had an even harder time relating to the prosthetics than they did to no arms at all. They called me names like "Robot Girl" and "Captain Hook."

When I got a little older, I branched out in some ways. I danced. I did some modeling when I was twelve and thirteen years old. I entered and won a Miss Valentine pageant. As a teen, I did some risky things. I hate to say it, but I was a pretty bad driver. I had some really good friends, but deep down I was still angry that I was different.

It wasn't until the first day of eighth grade that things really started to change.

No More Fake Arms

We moved to the big city of Tucson, Arizona, the summer before I started eighth grade. For me, it was a chance to make a fresh start. No one in the city knew me. I could be who I wanted to be.

I wanted to be the real Jessica. And the real Jessica didn't wear fake arms.

So on that first day of eighth grade, I carefully picked out my clothes. I shaved my legs for the first time. And I left my prosthetic arms in the closet.

As I walked out the door to the bus stop, I felt elated. At fourteen years old, leaving those fake arms behind was the most empowering thing I'd ever done. I was making a statement. I was Jessica, the way she is! Not "Jessica without arms," because I wasn't missing anything. I was who I was, and it just happened that I didn't have arms.

I was declaring myself to be the person God created me to be. It was my first solo as the pilot in command of me. And it marked the first step of being able to help others take flight in their lives, as well.

The Dreamers

I gave my first speech when I was a sophomore in high school.

I delivered it to a group of seventh graders called "The Dreamers." The Dreamers were underprivileged students sponsored by a philanthropist who wanted to encourage them to go to college or do whatever it was they dreamed of doing.

They brought me in to inspire The Dreamers. Someone dropped me off at the junior high school, and I spoke to the kids. I didn't really have a plan. *Just tell them about your life,* I told myself. *Tell them a little bit about how you do things.*

And sure enough, one at a time, they started to come up to me and tell me how inspired they were. I realized that my not having arms resonated with their own challenges in life. They connected with me immediately.

And I thought, *Wow, if I get this type of reaction just from sharing a little bit about my life, maybe I should do this more often.*

Speak Up

That was the start of my speaking career.

Speaking brought me out of my shell. It helped me to be okay with me, and it made me more extroverted. I wasn't just inspiring others by talking about my life. Somehow, sharing my story was like therapy for me. It helped me as much as it helped the people I talked to.

In college, I started out as a pre-med major, and pre-med changed to psychology my junior year. But by my senior year in college, I knew what I really wanted to do. I decided to pursue motivational speaking as a career. And right after I graduated, a front-page article came out in the *Arizona Daily Star*—the biggest newspaper in Tucson—with the headline "Armless Student Seeks to Be Motivational Speaker." Everybody saw it.

The whole thing took off from there. And I never looked back.

Your Formula for Taking Flight

One of the first things you have to learn as a pilot is the formula for flight.

The formula for straight and level flight looks pretty simple: lift = weight, and thrust = drag. Lift is the upward force created by the plane's wings moving through the air. Weight is the oppositional force of gravity. Thrust powers the plane to move forward. And drag is the resistance you come up against in flight—in particular, the airflow around the wings and body of the aircraft. But things like the plane's antenna or the aerodynamics of the airframe also affect drag.

To keep the aircraft in straight and level flight, those are the four basic factors that need to be balanced.

The formula for flight isn't just for pilots. You experience lift, weight, thrust, and drag all the time in your own life. Some things push you forward. Others seem to hold you back. You have experiences that lift you up and others that weigh you down. And when you strike the right balance between all these different things, you feel like you're at the top of your game, winging your way to success.

The flight formula is for you. You are looking to make your life take off in physical, emotional, and spiritual ways. And once you know the formula and the qualities that go into it, you can take flight in ways you never imagined.

The formula for flight in your life includes adventure, desire, courage, innovation, balance, persistence, support, authenticity, and faith.

ADVENTURE. Adventure is part of the "thrust" element in the flight formula. Your sense of adventure is what adds zest to your life. It keeps you discovering new things and inspires you to take full advantage of the opportunities that cross your path.

DESIRE. Desire is also about "thrust" in the formula for flight. If you don't have the desire to accomplish a certain goal, you will not have the thrust to follow through with it and make it happen. True desire pushes you to achieve your dreams.

COURAGE. Courage enters the formula for flight at the same time that "weight" does, because it is the force you use to combat fear. Sometimes, your fears can weigh you down. You might have a fear of failure or inadequacy, and that can stop you from taking flight. Your courage is what you use to overcome those fears and keep moving forward.

INNOVATION. Innovation is one thing that helps you conquer "drag" in the formula for flight. You use innovation to overcome the many obstacles and challenges you face. As long as you have ingenuity, resourcefulness, and creativity, you can find a way to make things work.

BALANCE. Balance is the second element of "weight" in the flight formula. Without balance in our lives, we feel weighted down and out of sync. To achieve success, you need a good sense of physical, emotional, and spiritual balance.

PERSISTENCE. Like innovation, persistence is another powerful force that helps you overcome "drag" in the formula for flight.

Facing failure is just part of life, and everyone goes through it. Ultimately, you can overcome failure with persistence.

SUPPORT. Support is the first factor of "lift" in the flight formula. Your family, friends, community, mentors, teachers, and so many others lift you up when you need it most. They give you the support you need to take flight.

AUTHENTICITY. Just like support, authenticity is an aspect of the formula for flight that "lifts" you up. When you are authentic with yourself and others, you lift yourself up to new levels of clarity, truth, and purpose.

FAITH. Finally, faith is the ultimate component of "lift" in the flight formula. Even in your most difficult moments, faith gives you the lift you need to make it through and carry on. The most difficult journey of my life was my journey to faith; and it was also the most rewarding one.

True flight requires every one of these factors. You have to have a good amount of desire and adventure—the thrust. You have to push through setbacks and obstacles—the drag—by learning how to persist and innovate. Then you have to use courage and balance to deal with the weight of what's holding you down so that it doesn't stop you from achieving your dreams. And finally, you have to lift yourself to success and propel yourself to the next horizon with support, authenticity, and faith.

These are the qualities I developed throughout my personal experiences, and they have strengthened me to be the person I am today: a pilot in command of my own outcomes. In these chapters, I'll show you how each of them played out in my life and, more importantly, how they have the power to inspire flight in yours.

When you take all the components of the formula for flight into account, you empower yourself to soar to new possibilities. You can set any challenge for yourself, and overcome it. You can disarm any obstacle you face and reach any goal you can imagine.

You can give yourself the ability to take flight in your life. And flight begins with the inner spark that makes you want to throttle down the runway in the first place: a sense of adventure.

Taken during my SCUBA certification course.

2

Thrust toward Adventure

Life is either a daring adventure or nothing.

~HELEN KELLER

Ready for Takeoff

RIGHT AROUND THE TIME I graduated from college, I was invited to speak in front of a Rotary Club in Tucson, Arizona.

This was in August 2005. My speaking career was just beginning. So that first week of August, I went to the club to deliver my speech. The room was filled with close to two hundred Rotary members. I shared my life story; I did a little taekwondo demonstration. On the whole, it went really well.

After the speech, a fighter pilot came up to me. His name was Robin Stoddard, and he represented a nonprofit organization called Wright Flight. Wright Flight is named after the Wright brothers—the founders of aviation. This nonprofit uses flying to inspire children to reach their goals. A child sets a goal, and when that goal is reached, he or she has the opportunity to go on a joyride in a single-engine airplane.

Robin Stoddard walked up to me and said, "Jessica, that speech was really inspiring. How would you like to go on a flight with us? I can't just give it to you. You will have to earn it just like the other Wright Flight participants. But I'd like you to have this opportunity."

I was terrified of flying. Even on commercial airplanes, I used to step foot in the door and just start praying for God to take care of me until I was on solid ground again.

But when Robin Stoddard came up to me that day, something sparked in me that was stronger than fear. It was a determination not to let opportunity pass me by.

It was a sense of adventure.

"Okay, what do I have to do?" I asked.

He assigned me a paper about disabled pilots in aviation, which I wrote. My first time in the air with Wright Flight turned into my first flying lesson. And, just like that, I put myself on the flight path to what would become one of the biggest adventures of my life.

The Spirit of Adventure

Adventure is the spice of life. It's about accepting opportunity when it crosses your path and never thinking twice about it. When you accept opportunity, you propel yourself to new heights. That's what makes adventure so important to the "thrust" element of the flight formula.

The opportunities for adventure that come your way may not always be things you already like to do. I personally did not like flying. But I recognized the invitation from Wright Flight as the opportunity it was, and I didn't want to let it pass me by.

You have to be willing to try new things, even though you think you might not like them. You have to be open to possibilities. That openness to possibilities is synonymous with being adventurous.

When you are adventurous, you face challenges that you've never been confronted with before, and those challenges expand your horizons. You gain a new perspective on life. Everything feels richer than it did before, and you appreciate things in a different way. Without adventure, life is dull and predictable. You are hardly ever excited to wake up in the morning, and you don't have nearly as many opportunities to learn and grow.

Adventure doesn't always have to be about things like African safaris or skydiving. You can bring adventure into your life even in an office setting. Maybe that means accepting a new position when someone offers it to you. Maybe it means putting a system in place that you've never tried before.

Adventure is a willingness to leave behind the predictable and thrust forward to something that is different. When you embrace adventure, you invite horizons into your life that you might not have even known existed. You challenge yourself in ways you never could have expected. And you learn things about yourself that, otherwise, you never would have known.

Dive into Adventure

One adventure often leads to the next. You may never get to experience all the adventures that life has to offer you if you don't say "yes" to that first opportunity.

When I was five years old, we had a swimming pool in our backyard. I didn't know how to swim, and the pool was well-fenced off. I never really thought twice about it.

Then one day, my aunt, who was living with us at the time, went swimming in the pool. And once she was in there, she started encouraging me to jump in, too. "I'll catch you," she called. "Come on, Jessica. Jump!"

The idea of jumping in the pool made me nervous. But my sense of adventure pushed me to do it. I braced myself and leapt into the water with both feet. I felt the impact of the water as I broke through the surface; then came the haunting uncertainty of whether I'd be able to come back up, once I was fully immersed.

But I did come back up to the surface. I was fine. Even better, I was having fun. And I found myself wanting more.

That first leap into the backyard pool led to a bigger leap from the city pool high dive a few years later. Then, in 2009, another adventure came my way: the opportunity to become SCUBA certified.

Just like flying, SCUBA certification wasn't necessarily something on my bucket list. I have to admit, being that far down in the water wearing all that equipment didn't sound like my cup of tea. But it was something new. It was adventurous. So I said, "Well, why not?"

I signed on with the organization that brought it to my attention, Diveheart. Diveheart helps people with disabilities get SCUBA certified. They invited me out to Downers Grove near Chicago, where I learned how to dive in the pool. We figured out the logistical challenges. I learned how to use my foot to clear water out of my mask. I figured out how to swim with one fin, dolphin-style, so that I could keep one foot free to control everything else.

Once that was settled, we went out to a quarry about an hour away from Downers Grove, Illinois, so that I could do the four dives I needed to get my certification.

The adventure of doing those dives was more than I could have imagined. I felt a sense of weightlessness—the thrill of not knowing what you're going to see next. I had experienced the air as a pilot, but SCUBA diving opened my eyes to an underwater world I hadn't even thought about before. *Wow, I didn't realize how much fun this was!* I thought.

And it all started with that first leap into the swimming pool when I was five.

You don't always know what an adventure will be like before you say "yes" to it. That's what makes it an adventure. You just have to dive in with both feet.

Adventurous Goals

A sense of adventure will bring new goals into your life. But it will also help you achieve the goals you already have.

I knew by the time I finished college that I wanted to be a motivational speaker. That was my goal. So when the opportunity to become a pilot came about, I didn't necessarily see right away how it would help me with my speaking. As far as I could tell, my speaking had brought me the adventure of learning how to fly. It wasn't going to work the other way around.

Well, it turns out that speaking and flying complement each other really well.

Becoming a pilot had a tremendous effect on my speaking career. It gave me experiences that became content for my speeches. More than that, it gave me a huge amount of credibility that I could not have attained otherwise. The goals and obstacles I faced in my journey to flight relate incredibly well to the goals and obstacles that the people I speak to face every day. When I talk about overcoming my fear of flying, they think about the fears they're facing in the present. When I talk about not giving up, they recognize that drive to persevere in themselves.

You may not always know how an adventure will help you achieve your current goals, and that's okay. Say "yes" to the adventure anyway. The results may surprise you. That's part of the fun.

Something Ventured, Something Gained

Even if you say "yes" to an adventure and it turns out to be a not-so-great experience, you will still get something out of it that will enrich your life.

When I was in college, I needed to pick up some kind of art credit to graduate. So I struck out on my own adventure: I signed up for a guitar class. I wasn't going to let not having arms stop me from trying to play the guitar. I wanted to experience something new.

And it just wasn't my thing. Sure, I could have found a way to create the chords in a new way so that I could play them with my toes. That wasn't the problem. The problem was that I didn't feel the spark of desire for it that I felt for other things. I didn't fall in love with it. So I didn't pursue the guitar, and I'm not a guitarist today.

But something else came out of that adventure that changed my life.

Before I took that guitar class, I was on my way to becoming a doctor. I was focused on getting into med school, and I spent all my time on one side of the University of Arizona campus, in the same group of buildings. The main building that I spent most of my time in looked like a hospital. The hallways were always quiet and sterile; there was no dirt on the ground. People walked around like they were on a mission. They went straight to the room they needed to be in, shut the door, and got to work.

Well, the first time I walked into the music building on the other side of campus, it was like entering a different world. People were just hanging out in the hallways, chatting up a storm. Everywhere I went, I heard music and laughter. All the doors were wide open. There wasn't any of the seriousness I was used to in the pre-med building. The music students were a lot more relaxed.

Wow, I thought, *I want to be more like these people.* I wanted to be free-spirited and relaxed like they were, instead of being driven all the time like the pre-med students. I wanted to enjoy the moment.

In my third year of college, I changed my major to psychology. It wasn't just because of that experience with the music students. But meeting them expanded the horizon of what I wanted for myself, and even today, that free-spirited nature is part of how I live my life.

Even though I didn't love playing the guitar, my adventure brought me something even more valuable in the end.

Adventure in Flight

Adventure brings you unexpected opportunities, and those opportunities bring zest to your life. Even if you feel uncertain at first, once you accept the adventures that come your way, you will disarm limits you never realized were there and open yourself to a world of possibilities that you hadn't even thought about before. And that will make your life richer than you could have ever imagined.

The first leap into adventure is the hardest part. But as the pilot in command of you, you need to take that leap. Once you do, you will catch a big lift to success and that next horizon—and you will thank yourself for it.

A leap into adventure can be the takeoff to amazing new heights. But it's not enough just to leave the ground. After you're in the air, you need a driving force that pushes you to keep gaining altitude. A big part of that force is desire—the next element in the formula for taking flight in life.

"Walls are only there
to stop the people who don't
want it badly enough."

~RANDY PAUSCH

Using nunchakus during a taekwondo class.

3

Desire: The Thrust to Reach Your Dreams

A shot glass of desire is greater than a pitcher of talent.

~ANDREW MUNTHE

TV Thief

DURING COLLEGE, I MOVED out of my parents' house and into an apartment with two roommates I had met through taekwondo. The apartment we found was perfect. It had three bedrooms and one bathroom, and it was right across from our stadium. We brought together all of the furniture we could find to furnish it, but one thing was missing.

We didn't have a TV.

I knew that my parents had three TVs in their house. *Hey, they can probably spare me one,* I thought. So I called my mom. "Mom, can I please borrow a TV just until my roommates and I can afford to get one?" I asked.

"Sure," she said, "that's fine. Just go home and check with your dad."

I went home to check with my dad. At the time, he was retired, and he was a big fan of watching TV. "Dad, can I borrow a TV until my roommates and I can afford to get one?" I asked. It was the same question I had asked my mom. But my dad had a different response.

He looked at me and said, "I don't know about that."

When my dad says, "I don't know about that," what he really means is, "No."

That wasn't the answer I wanted to hear. But I wasn't going to give up that easily. I was determined to get a TV for my roommates and me. *Okay,* I said to myself, *I have to figure out a way to get this TV out of the family room without my dad knowing.*

I waited until he went outside to water the plants. Then I made my move.

The TV I went after wasn't a nice, light, flat-screen TV. It was one of those box TVs, bulky and heavy. I hurried around to the back of it and unplugged the cords and the cable connecting it to the wall.

Then I had to figure out how to actually move it.

I need something to help me maneuver it out the door, I thought. I found a computer chair and wheeled it over to the TV. Then I went behind the TV and I pushed it 30 percent of the way off its stand with my foot. After that, I came around in front again. I hugged the TV with my right leg, standing on my left leg for balance. Then I pulled the TV onto the computer chair.

The TV was actually bigger than the chair. I knew if I made a wrong move, it would come crashing down. So I hovered over it, using my shoulders and my chin to hold it in place on the seat. With my feet, I slowly pushed the chair along the carpet. I made it through the TV room. Once I hit the kitchen tile, it was a lot easier to push.

But it wasn't over yet. I still had to make it down one big step on the way to the garage.

How am I going to get this thing down without toppling the TV? I thought. The answer was "one wheel at a time." Somehow, I managed to maneuver the chair down the step. The TV didn't fall. All I had left to do was get it over one last little bump and out the door, into the garage. My car was right on the other side.

By now, I was pouring sweat. This was August in Tucson, Arizona, and it was 110 degrees Fahrenheit outside. But I didn't care. I was driven by my desire to get this TV for my roommates and me. Nothing was going to stop me. Success was so close I could taste it. I opened up the garage door, elated.

Someone was standing there on the other side. It was my dad.

He looked at me and saw the sweat dripping down my face—the strain, the conviction, and the desire in my face to get that TV. And he said, "Honey, if I knew you wanted it that bad, I would have helped you."

His original answer might have been "I don't know about that." But through the sheer desire I demonstrated that day, I changed his "no" into a "yes."

The Power of Desire

If you want something badly enough, you'll figure out a way to do it—even if it means moving a TV without arms.

Desire is a key part of learning to take flight. It's part of the "thrust" element of the flying formula—the power that pushes you forward. Before you can accomplish anything, you first have to set the goal of doing it. Desire is what propels you to achieve that goal once you have it in your mind. It gives you the fuel you need to actually do the thing you've decided to do. Without that desire, you won't have what it takes to pursue your goal.

I have two black belts and a state champion title in the ATA, the largest taekwondo association in the United States. We have an acronym in taekwondo for goal setting: "SMART" goals. That stands for: specific, motivating, achievable, relevant, and trackable. Everyone in the ATA learns about SMART goals. You test your goal against each of those characteristics to see how strong it is, and it works really well.

I do even better using my own system. I simply visualize my goal. I put all my focus on wanting it enough. You have to truly desire the thing you want to accomplish. Desire fuels the persistence you need to keep you from giving up along the way.

If you want something enough, then you envision it. If you envision it, then you start believing that it's possible. And when you really start to believe something is possible, you act on it.

Write It Down, Make It Real

Desire makes an impact on your life when you can find real ways to apply it to what you're doing. One thing you can do to move from envisioning your goals to acting on them is to write down those goals.

In August 2013, I wrote down a goal. I physically wrote down with my foot that I wanted to become the ATA State Champion in Forms in Arizona for my division in the regular taekwondo ring—not the one for special abilities. All throughout the process of chasing this goal, from the day I decided to pursue it in August 2013 until May 2014, when they announced that I was state champ, I had a vision: I envisioned the back of my uniform saying "State Champ" in big black letters.

I wrote down that goal. I envisioned what it would look like. And sure enough, it became a reality.

Visualization also helped me on my journey to become a pilot. Getting my sport pilot certification was a three-year process, and at the lowest moment in my pilot training, I felt as though everyone had given up on the possibility that I could do it. I had already trained in three airplanes, and neither of them was functional for me.

That was the point in my career as a student pilot when I said, "If I want to make this goal a reality, I'm going to have to envision myself accomplishing it. I have to know what it would look like." The drag was threatening to stop me in my tracks. I needed to add more thrust.

So I pulled up a picture of the type of airplane that I wanted to fly and put it on my computer desktop. Every morning when I woke up, the first thing I did was turn on that computer and see that picture of the airplane I was going to fly. That allowed me to envision myself flying that airplane. I closed my eyes and imagined myself flying that exact model.

Sure enough, seven months after I made that vision part of achieving my goal, I was a certified pilot. When you visualize, the power of desire can take you to incredible heights.

Deserve It

Another part of using desire to help you achieve your goals is believing that you *deserve* to attain the thing that you desire in the first place. It sounds simple, but this is actually a very powerful tool.

When I was a sophomore in high school, I was in a beauty pageant sponsored by the Filipino-American community that I grew up with in Tucson. There were seven girls trying for the title of Miss Valentine, but I was the one who actually got it. I was so proud to make that title mine, but when I won it, I needed to know that it was rightfully mine—because of who I was as a person, and not out of sympathy for me not having arms.

So I looked at the judges' score sheets. Every contestant got a score for poise, or personality, and a few other attributes. Then those individual scores were added up to determine the pageant winner.

What I saw when I looked at those score sheets was that I earned the title fair and square. The score of the runner-up was just a couple of decimal points below mine. If there had been a big discrepancy, I'd have wondered where that was coming from; maybe favoritism or pity had come into play. Because the scores were so close, though, I was able to reassure myself that my win wasn't based on my disability.

Winning the title of Miss Valentine was an incredible life experience, but I remember afterwards hearing negative chatter from people. Word got back to me that someone said, "Oh, it was really unfair that she was in the pageant with all those other girls, because the judges were clearly going to favor her since she didn't have arms."

I knew that I had rightfully won my title, but it hurt knowing there was someone out there saying these things. It was upsetting to know that, rather than believe I could be fully deserving of earning that title on my own merits, someone assumed I had won merely out of pity.

But that was also a defining moment for me, because it forced me to stop and think. *Is this what my life is always going to be about?* I asked myself. *Am I always going to have to fight these people who doubt whether I deserve something?*

In the end, I realized that it didn't matter whether other people believed I deserved it. I knew that I deserved it. That was what counted most.

In life, no matter who you are or what challenges you face, you will meet naysayers along the path to your goal. But you can't let those people rain on your parade. You have to enjoy the moment. Acknowledge that your desire and your commitment earned you your goal. No one can take that away from you.

Desire in Flight

So many people feel unworthy of being the pilot in command of their own success. They let the baggage of unworthiness bog down their desire to achieve their goals. It comes up as that little nagging voice in the back of your head that says, "Can I even do this?"

You might hear that voice sometimes. When that happens, instead of giving in to it, let it challenge you. Allow it to propel you toward your goal—your next horizon. At first, this may seem counterintuitive, but you'll realize soon enough how powerful a tool this can be.

Remember that desire is what initiates any kind of goal that you set. You first have to want to do it. If your heart isn't in it, you won't be able to move past the inevitable hurdles you'll face along the way.

I love the Randy Pausch quote "Walls are only there to stop the people who don't want it badly enough." It's true. If you don't want something enough, then in every hurdle you'll find another excuse to stop you from doing what it is you love or want to do. But if you want something badly enough, you won't let those little obstacles—or even big ones—keep you from taking flight. Instead, you'll disarm your limits and figure out a way to make it down the runway anyway, in spite of all odds.

Your desire does more than just fuel your goals. It's also the spark that leads you to the next principle you need in the formula for flight: courage.

My first dance recital.

4

The Weight of Courage

Identify your greatest fear and walk directly at it.

~ELEANOR ROOSEVELT

The Flying Samaritans

MY FIRST OPPORTUNITY TO do an international keynote speech required a two-hour trip in a single-engine airplane. And when I found out about the plane, let me tell you, I wasn't exactly jumping up and down for joy.

The speech opportunity itself was really exciting. It came through a volunteer group called The Flying Samaritans, an organization that offers free medical clinics for the underprivileged. They were having their annual conference, and they asked me to come speak to their medical volunteers in San Carlos, Mexico.

I was really looking forward to everything about it—except the plane ride. Flying was one of my biggest fears. I didn't even like flying on commercial planes, and this little single-engine airplane looked even scarier. It was true that a few weeks before at the Rotary Club meeting, Robin Stoddard had invited me to fly with Wright Flight, but that flight hadn't taken place yet. The opportunity to fly down to speak to the Samaritans came up at the last minute.

Oh man, I don't know if I really want to do this, I thought. But what I *did* really want to do was give that keynote speech. This was 2005, and I was twenty-one years old. My career was just starting. The Flying Samaritans gig was not only going to be my first international keynote, but also my first keynote speech ever, period.

I decided to face down my fear. On October 21, 2005, I said a prayer and set foot in a small plane for the first time in my life.

I thought it would be worse than commercial planes, but I was wrong. It actually turned out to be a little easier, because I was in the copilot seat, so I could see what was going on. I saw the whole control panel. I saw the pilot using the controls. *Wow,* I thought, *this is actually kind of cool.*

I survived the flight to Mexico and gave my speech to The Flying Samaritans. That was a great experience. After it was over, I had to get back on the single-engine airplane and fly home. We took off, no turbulence, no problems. I was less terrified than I'd been the first time.

Then, about thirty minutes into the flight, the pilot turned to me and said, "How'd you like to feel what it's like to have your foot on the yoke?"

The yoke in an airplane is like the steering wheel in a car. The possibility of touching the yoke had never even crossed my mind. I looked at him and then at the controls. I was in the copilot's seat again, so everything that was in front of him was also in front of me. I knew the plane was on autopilot; there was no danger of crashing. "Okay," I said.

I put my foot on the yoke.

The feeling of moving the controls on that single-engine airplane as it cut through the sky was incredible. It was exhilarating. That was the moment when I made one of the biggest commitments of my life: the commitment to overcome my fear.

I was going to become a pilot.

The Courage to Take Flight

My commitment to become a pilot was an act of courage.

Your fears can weigh you down. They can keep you from reaching for your full potential. Courage means moving forward in the face of those fears. It means taking that next step toward your dreams, even when you know that you might have to backtrack.

Courage is what pushes you through that critical moment of doubt and opens the doors you want to soar through as the pilot in command of your own life. Without courage, you never reach beyond what is safe and comfortable. You don't feel the pride and confidence that comes with taking on new challenges, and you never experience the power of your full potential.

Many people who face challenges in life have a tendency to go backwards. They use their challenge as a scapegoat for not doing something. And everyone else feels okay with that. "Oh, that person is at a disadvantage," they say. "It's okay." Then they pat the person on the head and send that individual on his or her way, no problem.

But no challenge you face is ever a match for courage. Here's one example. When I was in elementary school, we had a baseball team. Without arms, I could have gotten out of that game easily. I had a good excuse. But I also had courage, and I didn't want to be an outsider looking in, watching everyone else in class play while I sat on the sidelines.

So I figured out a way that I could still participate. Someone stood in as the batter for me, and that allowed me to run the bases. I refused to use the obstacle of not having arms as a scapegoat. I had the courage to step up and play the game in a way that it had never been played before. And it became a wonderful experience.

Courage is something we all need, whether or not you have a disability. For every moment that I reached the tipping point of a decision and had the courage to follow through, an old fear died and a new opportunity was born. I became addicted to that moment of overcoming my deepest, heaviest fears. And that shaped my life in ways I never imagined.

Once you taste courage, you keep wanting more.

The High Dive of Courage

It is really true that one act of courage gives you the power to undertake a bigger act of courage in the future.

I told you in chapter 2 about my decision to jump in our family swimming pool when I was five. That jump was a leap into adventure, but it was also an act of courage. And it led to an even bigger act of courage five years later, when I was ten: jumping off the city pool high dive.

The high dive at that public swimming pool was ten feet above the water. I was there for swimming lessons, and all of us in the class viewed that dive as a rite of passage. The high dive was a pretty big feat for any child, and it was even more difficult for me because of the ladder. Even though the ladder was angled a little bit, my mom was still worried that I could fall off and get hurt trying to climb it without arms. She didn't want me to jump off the high dive for that reason.

But I wasn't going to let that ladder stop me. I was enrolled in swimming lessons with my friend, and one day my mom didn't drive us to the pool. She set it up so that my friend's mother would take us there instead. Well, that was my cue. My mother wasn't there to stop me. This was going to be the day.

"I want to go up the high dive," I told my swim instructor.

"Okay . . . " he said. "Well, here's what we can do. I'm going to be close behind you on the ladder, just in case you slip and fall back. But I'm not going to help you up that ladder."

"Sure," I agreed. "Yeah. That's how I plan to do it."

We headed over to the high dive, and I started climbing the ladder. My feet did the usual thing, and I used my chin and shoulder to pull myself up and keep my balance. Step by step, I edged my way up to the very top of the ten-foot dive. Everything was just fine . . . until I climbed over that last step.

I looked down, and my stomach turned into jelly. It was *really* high.

I glanced back. My swim coach had been behind me all the way up the ladder, but he wasn't there anymore. As soon as I reached the top, he'd gone back down. *What did I just get myself into?* I thought.

I stood up there on the platform for a while, torn. Way down below, the other kids from my class were looking up at me. They seemed so much smaller than they did when I was on the same level with them. Even the water looked more terrifying than it had when I was swimming in it, just a few minutes earlier.

Wow . . . I thought. And that was when the courage came through. *Well, I got myself up here. I guess I actually have to do this.*

I stepped toward the edge of the board. My sensitive feet absorbed how hot and rough it felt, like sandpaper. I took a deep breath.

I jumped.

I went straight into the water with my legs together, like a pencil. It was actually an advantage not to have arms in the way; I didn't have to figure out what to do with them. It still hurt to hit the water, though. The plunge to the bottom of the pool felt like it went on forever, and for a moment I panicked. *Am I going to make it back up to the surface?*

I did make it up. Relief and adrenaline rushed through me. I'd done it. I had gone through the rite of passage. More than that, I had tasted the rewards of courage.

Years later, I took that same courage to greater heights. I skydived. I learned how to fly a plane. My courage just took me higher and higher, to more and more satisfying rewards. That's how courage works.

Small Acts, Big Courage

Courage doesn't always have to mean life or death. It isn't always about skydiving and physical danger. Sometimes, the smallest things we do can be our biggest acts of courage.

As I mentioned in chapter 1, when I was a sophomore in high school, my friends decided to enter a Miss Valentine beauty pageant. So I decided I'd do it with them. It sounded like fun, and I wanted to be part of the experience.

Then I heard that part of the pageant was a bathing suit competition.

Oh no, I thought. *That's not for me. There is no way I'm doing that.* During my insecure teen years, I wasn't even comfortable wearing a swimsuit in my own swimming pool with no one around but my friends, unless I had a T-shirt over it.

It wasn't just my armlessness that made me self-conscious. I also had muscular thighs and a big butt because I used my legs for everything, so they were more built than the average girl's. In fact, at sixteen, I was more insecure about my butt and my "thunder thighs" than I was about my armless shoulders! The vulnerability of being exposed in a bathing suit in front of two or three hundred people seemed impossible to overcome.

In the end, it became a test of courage. Could I really do this? Could I stand up there on that stage in front of all those people and a panel of judges? There was no skipping the bathing suit portion. I had to do everything, or I couldn't be in the pageant at all. I knew one thing for sure: I'd rather be on the inside going through this experience with my friends than on the outside not taking part at all.

I decided to follow through with it.

I remember how naked I felt even during the rehearsal—the chill of the air conditioning on my bare skin. I told myself I could get through it. I watched the other girls out there doing their best, and I was determined not to let my fear stop me.

Then the night of the pageant arrived, and I found myself backstage in my bathing suit, standing behind the curtain, waiting to be announced.

That was the moment when it really hit me that there was a clear line. On my side of the curtain, it was dark and anonymous. On the other side, there were spotlights. There were judges and cameras and hundreds of pairs of eyes.

I realized that I didn't have to go out there. I could stay backstage in the shadows, where it was safe. Or I could cross that threshold of darkness into the light and show myself to the world in my most vulnerable state. I pulled together all the courage I could.

The moment I stepped out from behind the curtain, I held my breath. I knew that everyone could see everything about me, and I was totally exposed. It felt just like jumping off the high dive when I was ten. The light had touched me, and there was no going back.

Okay, I told myself, *you're past the point of no return now. There's no more holding back, so you might as well just strut your stuff.*

And I did. I walked down the modeling path, over to the center of the stage, down the steps. I strode with confidence; none of the insecurity I felt a moment before came with me. I traveled the whole circuit, designed so the audience could see you. Then I made it back up to the stage, did the little turn we were supposed to do, and finally disappeared behind the curtain again.

Once I was back there, I realized: I had done it. I had survived. Not only had I survived, but I was proud of myself. I had put forth confidence in the face of my fear, and that was very self-affirming.

When you carry yourself with courage, the challenges you are able to overcome will surprise you.

The Courage to Dance

Courage isn't just about making it through life's tough moments. When you act with courage, you can open your eyes to new opportunities and new ways to enjoy life.

When I was five years old, my mom decided to put me in dance lessons. She wanted to expose me to the world and encourage me not to hold back, even though I was different. The class we picked was tap dancing, and it did help me open up a little bit. But what I didn't anticipate was that, at the end of the year, we would have a dance recital.

The idea of the recital didn't sit well with me at all. I pictured myself on stage in front of my friends and family, bright light in my eyes, tap dancing for the world to see. Even as a five-year-old, I knew that I wanted nothing to do with that. At that age, I wasn't insecure about my butt and thighs yet, but I was insecure about the fact that I was different.

So I resolved not to do it. Instead, I decided that I would manipulate my mother into talking to the dance teacher for me. "Jessica is not doing the recital," she'd say. "She thinks it's a great idea and everything, but she's not going to do it." And my mother did talk to the dance teacher, just like I wanted her to.

But the dance teacher wasn't going to let me off the hook that easily.

I watched the two of them discuss it in hushed voices. When they came back to me, they didn't exactly tell me whether or not I'd been excused from the performance. "You know, Jessica, we're just going to buy your costume," my mom said. "All the other little girls are getting fitted for their costumes."

"Okay, fine," I agreed. "We'll buy a costume." I figured it would be a great souvenir for the year.

That was the first step of their secret plan. I got fitted for the costume—bright pink with a little tutu—and I loved it. Then they started working on me. "Okay Jessica, why don't you do this dance?" and "You know, Jessica, you're really going to miss out if you don't do the recital." I started to waver. I said I would do it as long as I could be in the back row.

"But there isn't going to be a back row," my dance teacher said. And I knew what that meant. It was going to be me, right up there in front with all the other kids—just like I feared.

I did the recital anyway.

I remember being led out to my marker on the dark stage. Then the lights came on, and I saw the reality of where I was: surrounded by a huge auditorium filled with people. I immediately dropped my gaze to stare straight down at the floor. The music started playing, and we did the first couple of tap moves.

Then, all of a sudden, I heard a round of applause. A little bit of courage sparked in me. Slowly, I started to raise my eyes and look up, out at the people. The audience was cheering and clapping, just thrilled with the dancers—including me. They were happy and encouraging. To me, that was an affirmation. I wasn't supposed to sit out the recital or stay in the shadows.

I belonged here with the other girls. Dancing in the light.

Because of that experience, I made it through more than that one performance. I danced for twelve years. Dancing brought joy to my life, and it broadened my horizons. I wanted to get back on stage. I wanted to be in the spotlight.

Later, when I reached adulthood, I realized that all those years on stage also had a larger purpose: they prepared me for a career as a professional speaker. I was learning how to be comfortable with my difference in the public eye. That gave me not only confidence, but also the foundation I needed to be able to turn my situation into a positive force for helping other people.

The things you fear can be enormous blessings. All you need is the courage to look up.

Courage in Flight

Courage is one of the most powerful tools you have as the pilot in command of you. When the weight of your fears makes you want to retreat, courage is what helps you stay the course. It gives you the strength to acknowledge your mistakes and learn from them. Every act of courage you make, big or small, is a choice that will disarm your limits and keep you moving forward on the flight path to success.

Your courage to "look up" gives you the awareness to face life for what it is. When you look up, you can see the direction you want to go in. You become the pilot who determines the flight path of your life, and you realize that you really have what it takes to propel yourself to the next horizon.

Courage isn't the only part of the flight formula that can help you overcome turbulence in your life. Your creativity and resourcefulness can lift you to even greater heights. In the next chapter, I'll show you the power of innovation and how you can use it to tame the "drag" element of the formula for taking flight.

This is how I handle the controls in the airplane.

5

Think Outside the Shoe: Innovate to Overcome Drag

Necessity is the mother of invention.

~ANONYMOUS

Think Outside the Shoe

WHEN I WAS SIX years old, I had to learn how to tie my shoelaces like any other little kid.

I had to be able to do it myself, because I went to a public school. I didn't always have special help when it came to things like that. If my shoes came untied, there might not be anyone around to retie them for me. I had to depend on myself.

The actual tying part wasn't an issue. I used my toes to tie things all the time. The problem was this: How do you use your toes to tie your shoes, when your toes are *inside* the shoes you need to tie?

It took a while to figure this out, but in the end, I did it. Since my toes had to be out of the shoes to tie the laces, I learned to tie the laces first. I tied them loosely enough so that I could slide my feet into the shoes after they were tied.

That was how I first learned how to "think outside the shoe."

Years later, when I was starting my flight training, I found that I needed to wear a four-point harness. A four-point harness is fairly standard in the cockpit of most airplanes, but it had an added benefit for me because it kept me stable in the seat so that I could use both of my legs to fly.

The four-point harness secured me in place and gave me the leverage I needed to work the controls. But it presented the same problem that my shoelaces had fifteen years before: after you put it on, you have to fasten a bunch of complicated straps—straps I couldn't reach with my toes, once the harness was on my body.

Well, I thought, *I know what to do about this.*

I didn't put the harness on right away. Instead, I put the whole thing together with my feet first. Then I loosened the straps and slid my body into it, the same way I slid my six-year-old foot into my shoes, back on the playground at school. It was my first act of innovation in figuring out how to be a pilot—though it certainly wasn't the last.

Thinking outside the shoe helped me get my sport pilot certification. It can help you achieve amazing things, too.

The Need to Innovate

Innovation is stepping outside of the usual method of doing things and finding a completely different way to achieve the same end goal. It's connected to the "drag" element in the formula for flight, because you use it to overcome obstacles. In fact, innovation comes out of being confronted with a challenge that would otherwise drag you down. It's a truly invaluable tool when it comes to taking charge as the pilot in command of your own success.

At some point in your life, you will run into a situation where doing something the way everyone else does it is just not going to work for you. When that day comes, if you don't have innovation, your reaction is going to be, "Okay, I give up." You won't see the other options available to you.

But if you have innovation, your reaction to that situation is different. Instead of giving up, you say, "Well, wait a minute, maybe I can do this differently." Your eyes of innovation open you up to new possibilities, and you keep moving forward toward your dream of success.

Innovation doesn't happen inside a vacuum; it occurs in response to a need. You understand the need to innovate when you face a problem that doesn't have an obvious solution. That makes it a process. To innovate successfully, you have to identify the existing challenge to overcome. Then you have to look for an innovative solution and think about what function you ultimately need to accomplish.

The best part is that there will likely be more than one way to accomplish whatever needs to be done. Innovation is full of possibility. Your job is to think through those possibilities and identify the one that best fits your unique situation. You have to be creative. You have to see things from a different angle.

You have to think outside the shoe.

Innovation: The Key to the Skies

When you are willing to innovate, you bring your dreams within reach.

Learning how to put on a four-point harness was just one piece of the enormous jigsaw puzzle I put together when I became a pilot. I built every piece of that puzzle myself, using innovation.

The Ercoupe gave me a good place to start. Unlike other planes, it's the only one that can be flown without rudder pedals—which are usually located on the floor, where the brake pedal is in a car.

Instead, the Ercoupe's rudder is tied to the yoke, which is like the steering wheel. The yoke is unique because it pitches the aircraft up and down as well as simultaneously banking and turning it right and left. That eliminated the obstacle of needing limbs down on the floor and up on the controls at the same time. But it wasn't the only limit I had to disarm.

Reaching all of the controls was still one of my first challenges. I needed to be able to safely reach things like the throttle, the yoke, and the radio. One of the first things I realized was that I had to take my right foot off the yoke to turn knobs on the radio—which is important, because that's how you communicate with the other pilots in your airspace. But it's very unsafe when you don't have a limb on the yoke. I had to find another way to maintain physical contact with the yoke.

I couldn't use my left foot, because there wasn't enough space to fit it between the yoke and my torso. *Well,* I thought, *what if I put my left knee directly under the yoke?* But when I lifted my knee to do that, it didn't have support from the floor.

So I made the support I needed. I started with a phone book. I placed it on the floor under the yoke and used it as a place to brace my foot. The phone book later evolved into a wooden block built by one of the mechanics at the airport. The block kept my foot stable and let me maintain contact with the yoke at the same time.

I faced challenges like that more times than I can count when I was learning to fly. How could I reach every one of the controls on the panel with my feet? How would the seatbelt need to hold me to keep me safe when I landed? How would I unbuckle myself and pull myself out of the airplane if there was an emergency?

These were questions I had to answer. When I went for the check ride, which is like a driver's license test for pilots, the examiner wasn't going to say, "Oh, she doesn't have arms, so she doesn't have to buckle her own seatbelt. Someone else can buckle her in." Not by a long shot. I was held accountable for everything, which meant that not a single question could be left unanswered.

When that day came, I answered every last one of those questions, and countless others. I answered them with innovation. And by doing that, I turned a hand-and-arm-flying airplane into a foot-and-leg-flying airplane.

For me, flight training took more than reading the instruction manuals. It took an attitude of innovation, ingenuity, and creativity. There aren't many obstacles in life that you can't overcome with those things.

Daily Innovation

Innovation has the power to work miracles, but that doesn't mean it only happens on a grand scale. Some of the most important innovations in life are the ones we use in small ways in our daily life.

You may not realize it, but you've been innovating since childhood. There are things you've been doing all your life, like getting dressed and taking care of your personal needs, that you weren't born knowing how to do. You had to figure them out. You had to be creative. And that's the way it should be.

Most people I meet are more curious to find out how I go about doing my simple daily routines than how I fly an airplane. "How do you function on a daily basis?" they ask. From the moment I wake up, all the daily tasks that most people use their arms and hands for are different for me: getting dressed, using the restroom, taking a shower.

I had to learn how to do these kinds of things for myself when I was young, just like everybody else. But in my case, they required a little extra innovation and ingenuity, because I had to do them differently.

Ingenious Pants

It took me longer to learn how to get my pants up and down than it took me to learn how to fly an airplane.

When I was very young, independence wasn't absolutely necessary. But my mom knew that it was important for me to have a system in place so that when I grew older, I could be more independent.

That system started with Velcro. We sewed it onto my underwear and pants. Then we taped another strip of it onto the wall in the restroom. That way, while I was wearing them, I could attach my underwear or pants to that piece of Velcro and then move my legs, hips, and the rest of my body out of or back into the clothing as needed. It was a good idea, but trying to get dressed this way, I ended up tearing holes in my underwear and pants.

"We have to come up with a different idea," my mom said.

The "different idea" came from an occupational therapist of mine. She proposed a hook; the kind that you would normally put on the back of a door to hang a coat on. So we decided to give it a try. We bolted two hooks to the wall: one pointing down, and the other pointing up. With one hook, I maneuvered myself out of my pants, and with the other I put them on.

This system worked, too, but only at home. And we knew I wouldn't always be at home. We realized we needed to come up with yet another method for the pants—one that was more transportable.

That's when my occupational therapist came up with a new, improved solution to the problem: a hook that could be suctioned onto or off of the wall. She got the idea from a windshield repair tool and used her innovation to repurpose that idea for my pants. I could suction the hook onto the wall facing either up or down, depending on whether I was getting dressed or undressed. And best of all, it could travel with me when I wasn't home.

Essentially, this worked for putting on and removing pants in the same way that the first set of hooks worked—only because I could suction these hooks onto any smooth surface, I could travel with them and use them outside of my home.

The path to those suction hooks was a thirteen-year process. It took us that long to figure out exactly what kind of method would not only work best, but also be mobile and transportable. I use these hooks to this day. Because of this one innovative tool, I can be independent. I can use a public restroom by myself. I can travel the world as a motivational speaker.

One small piece of innovation has given me the life I live today. That's the power of everyday innovation.

" . . . How Do You Wipe?"

Putting on my pants isn't the only daily activity people ask me about. I get questions about the other basics of my day-to-day routines all the time.

Probably the number-one question I'm asked is how I use the toilet. I've even been asked about this on the radio. People call in, and they always want to know, "But . . . how do you wipe?" I actually just grab and hold toilet paper in the same way that most people use their hand. I roll the toilet paper and put it on my heel, and I bend my leg under me like a stork, so one foot is facing up. Then I just sit down on my heel to wipe. No problem.

The rest of my morning routine is just as simple. Shirts and bras are much easier to put on than pants. I just fasten the bra first and then pull it over my head like I do with the shirt—another instance of "thinking outside the shoe." I sit on a stool in the shower and wash my hair with my toes. I blow dry and brush my hair the same way: I just sit on a stool and hold the dryer and the brush with my foot.

The only real noticeable modification in our house is that there's a bar stool in the kitchen. I sit on the stool when I cook, wash dishes, and put things away. There is also a bar stool in the restroom. Nothing else looks any different from your average home. But innovation happens constantly beneath the surface.

Ongoing Innovation

To really put yourself on the flight path to success, you have to keep challenging yourself to stay innovative—even when you think you already know how to do something.

I once gave a keynote speech to a group of people at a company called Whirley-DrinkWorks in Pennsylvania. They had all their salespeople in a room for a weekend, and they brought me in to do the speech. Then they asked me if I could also do a workshop to open the salespeople's minds to new possibilities.

I'd never done a workshop, but I created one. And the topic of the hour was innovation.

Altogether, forty or so people were in the workshop. I broke them up into groups of eight, and I gave each group a station. The stations had different functions that the salespeople needed to accomplish—just simple things, like making a cup of coffee.

Once they were at their stations, I told them, "This is the only rule for this workshop: for the next hour, you cannot use your arms or hands. If you have an itch on the top of your head, you have to find some other way to scratch it. Everyone will get a chance to try all the stations. Go for it!"

I watched as the groups took on their challenges. The first group worked on making the cup of coffee. The second one had to open up a can of soda. The third group had to figure out how to put on a T-shirt, and the fourth station had to put on oversized pants. Finally, the fifth group was assigned to write a sentence on a piece of paper.

They loved it. They strategized together about how to overcome this hurdle or meet that challenge. It became a big brainstorming session as they determined which tactics helped, what kind of angles helped, what types of attitudes helped. They thought about life—and themselves—in a way they never had before.

Making a cup of coffee wasn't something they took for granted anymore. It was an act of innovation.

Innovate to Change the World

When you innovate, the benefits go beyond just you. Other people in the world are facing the same challenges you're facing. And when you "think outside the shoe," you can use your innovation to change the world.

One thing that I am passionate about is assisting children who have lost limbs or were born without them. I love giving back to them and their families, helping them figure things out the way I had to figure them out myself. My methods of innovation aren't always the easiest for them. But even when that's the case, my methods inspire them to keep innovating, themselves. So I keep sharing.

Even if you don't set out to help other people on purpose, you can still change the world with innovation, just by being who you are and doing what you do.

When I was ten years old, I was in a public park with my mother and siblings when we ran into a little girl who didn't have legs. She was about my age, and she used her arms and hands to compensate for not having legs, the same way I used my toes and legs to compensate for not having arms.

Of course, my mom immediately struck up a conversation with this girl's mother. "Oh yeah, she does everything," the mother said. "She's even in taekwondo!"

And my mom had this bright idea. *Why don't I bring my kids to taekwondo, too?* she thought.

So one day, my brother, my sister, and I all showed up at the taekwondo school. My brother and sister didn't stay for more than a couple of months. It wasn't their thing. But I loved it. Something about it just stuck with me.

So I stayed in that school for four years. I earned my first black belt when I was fourteen. I stopped for a few years when we moved to Tucson, but I took it up again when I went to college. It was a different style of taekwondo, so I had to relearn everything. As I learned, my instructors created new training and test requirements for me so that I could participate without arms.

By the time I received my second black belt, something great had happened: the ATA had created a completely new curriculum for people without arms. They officially integrated it into the system at the actual ATA headquarters. Today, anyone who doesn't have full use of their arms can join the ATA and fully participate using the curriculum that was initially developed for me.

I hadn't set out to change the way the system worked. But I changed it anyway, with innovation. Just by being me.

Innovation in Flight

If there's one thing to learn from innovation, it is this: you can be resourceful. One of the things you are constantly told as a pilot is, "Use your resources!"

No matter who you are, with any goal you pursue, you will come up against hurdles. Obstacles that seem like insurmountable challenges will present themselves, and you will ask yourself, "Can I really do this?" But that's not really the right question.

The correct question is: "How am I going to do this?"

You have what it takes to disarm your limits. You have resources available to you that you haven't even thought of yet. When you encounter drag in flight, figure out how to reduce or overcome it. Try looking at the obstacle or challenge in a different way, or from a different perspective. Most of the time, you'll come up with not just one but a variety of solutions. And the more solutions you come up with, the higher you can soar on your flight path to success.

As the pilot in command of you, you will always face obstacles and challenges. You have the power to get past these hurdles using your own ingenuity, creativity, and resourcefulness. That is the beauty of innovation.

Innovation will invite countless new opportunities into your world. Once you have them, you need to be able to keep them steady so that you don't get overwhelmed. In chapter 6, I'll take you through the next important part of the formula for flight: balance.

Walking down the aisle with Patrick on our wedding day.

6

Weightless: Perfect Balance

Happiness is not a matter of intensity, but of balance, order, rhythm, and harmony.

~THOMAS MERTON

On One Foot

I HAVE TO BE able to function while standing on one foot. So, not surprisingly, balance is a critical part of my life.

People often admire my perfect balance. But I developed this skill out of necessity. For example, when I'm at the grocery store and need to swipe my credit card, I stand on one leg while, with the other foot, I dig the card out of my purse, swipe it through the machine, and then sign the receipt.

I also stand on one foot to get my keys out of my purse, put the key in the lock, and open my front door. I have to balance actual items using my feet. If my cell phone starts ringing in my purse and I am in a public place, I'm usually standing. So I grab my phone with my right foot, once again standing on my left foot, and I manage to put my phone up to my ear in order to listen to it.

Without balance, I wouldn't be able to handle my normal, day-to-day life.

Find the Perfect Balance

Balance is that state of being where everything is working together in harmony. It's the homeostasis between the physical, mental, and spiritual attributes in your life. When you have perfect balance, you feel completely still and in tune with the forces around you. You can focus clearly on what you are doing. The moment you lose your focus, you lose your balance.

Balance is part of the "weight" element in the flight formula. It's a crucial component for maintaining straight and level flight. In order for an airplane to take flight, the center of gravity has to be in the right place. You need a specific balance of people, fuel, equipment, and cargo for that to happen. If any of those things pushes the center of gravity too far out of place, the other three elements of the flight formula—lift, thrust, and drag—stop working, and the plane can't fly.

Just like it does in an airplane, balance plays an incredibly important role in our daily movement through the world around us. If one force in your life is heavier or more powerful than another, it throws off your "center of gravity." That's why balance requires having a good idea of how powerful each force is. When you're aware of the weight of each element at all times, you empower yourself to counter them for straight and level flight.

The moment that an airplane is not in balance with the forces surrounding it—lift, weight, thrust, and drag—it can cause the pilot to lose control. In the same way, you have to maintain that kind of balance in your own life before you can be the pilot in command of your outcomes.

What are the things that have to be in balance for you to achieve flight?

A Balance of Responsibility

Balancing the different responsibilities of life isn't easy. But once you find a way to do it, your life itself becomes that much more rewarding.

One of the most challenging things for me, when I'm traveling the globe, is the simple rhythm of when to sleep, eat, and exercise. It doesn't sound like much, but when you're in one time zone one day and another time zone the next, that becomes an ongoing challenge. It's hard to keep myself in any kind of routine, but when I do, I feel better and I deliver better speeches. I am more effective as a motivational speaker.

Another challenge with working abroad and traveling so much is the need to balance work and family. My husband, Patrick, usually travels with me, so we get the benefit of being together more. My parents, on the other hand, want to see me more than they're able to with my work and travel schedule, and it's harder to find that balance of work and family time with them. I devote a lot of focus to prioritizing time with them and the rest of my family.

I'm also responsible for keeping up my internal balance. Internal balance is a mental state. If I'm out of balance internally, I sometimes feel insecure and I get caught off guard. When I'm in a situation where I feel that way, I know I'm not able to give my best performance. So I restore my internal balance by focusing my thoughts on the present moment. I let go of everything that's distracting me, and I concentrate on the vision of what I need to do. After I do that, my mind feels calm again.

Getting enough sleep is also a simple way to restore my internal balance. Without enough sleep, I'm groggy and tired, and I tend to attract a lot of attention in public that I don't want. But if I'm rested, I give off positive vibes, and that's exactly what I want to do. I'm not just a motivational speaker for an hour on stage once in a while. With internal balance, I can be that motivational speaker in my everyday encounters.

The trick is to be aware of what is necessary to keep your responsibilities—to others and to yourself—in balance. You have to balance the weight. Once you have your priorities in order, balance becomes a lot easier.

The Three Levels of Balance: Physical, Mental, Spiritual

Balance happens at three levels: physical, mental, and spiritual. If you really want to take advantage of true balance, you have to bring all three types into your life.

One thing that taught me the importance of the three levels of balance was taekwondo. In taekwondo, you can't succeed if you only have one kind of balance. You need the three types to achieve your full potential.

Physical balance is the obvious one. To participate in any martial art, you have to be physically fit and flexible. When you enter a sparring ring, your physical presence and energy need to be 100 percent there, in the moment. Without that physical presence, you're going to mess up. You could even get hurt. No one gets very far in taekwondo without developing physical balance.

You also need mental balance to succeed in taekwondo. Your mental balance is your focus. When you focus, you mentally prepare for what you want to do. You're in the zone, and that gives you self-control. If you go into a sparring ring without focus, your opponent will score on you because you won't see the attack coming. But if you have mental balance, you will be ready for anything an opponent throws at you. You will be able to react immediately, and that will give you the upper hand.

Finally, the best taekwondo masters also have spiritual balance. When you watch them, you can feel a presence even higher than their mental focus. That presence puts their physical and mental balance into perfect alignment. You can tell from their forms that they're in a natural flow of movement. They're not forcing things to happen. They feel a connection with something bigger than themselves, and they work together with that support to perform amazing martial arts.

These same principles apply to you as the pilot in command of your own success. Your physical balance will help you navigate the challenges of everyday life. Strong mental balance will keep you focused on what you want to achieve. And spiritual balance will take you to the next level. It will show you the bigger picture and give you a greater perspective on life.

When that happens, you will feel the three levels of balance working together in ways that you never could have imagined.

The Domino Effect

Physical, mental, and spiritual balance are all connected. When one of them is out of balance, it causes a domino effect that knocks the other two out of balance right along with it. And if you don't correct it right away, the imbalance gets worse and worse.

I once gave a speech to a legal firm of three hundred people in Kansas City, Missouri. It took me two hours to drive out there from Manhattan, Kansas, by myself in a rental car, and that was not an easy drive. The sun was beating down, and the wind was incredibly powerful. It felt like it was trying to blow my car off the road. I had to struggle with the steering wheel the entire time, fighting against the elements.

That put a lot of strain on me. By the time I arrived at the hotel where the event was being held, I was drained. I drove right past the entrance and had to circle back around. I was stiff, hungry, and thirsty. My physical balance was way off course.

But I didn't take the time to address it.

I don't have time to eat, I thought, *I don't have time to rest. I have to be on stage in twenty minutes, and I still have to review my talking points. The speech is more important. I'll get a snack and something to drink later.*

So I skipped physical balance and went straight to mental balance—the talking points of my speech. I ignored my physical state and went through everything I usually covered in my mind backstage, before a presentation. Before I knew it, they were announcing my name. A round of applause went up.

As soon as I set foot on that stage, I knew that something was wrong.

I felt overwhelmed. A headache pounded against my temples. My neck and shoulders were tense. I spoke all the words I usually said, but I had to think about them a little harder than usual. Normally I interact and make eye contact with a few members of the audience to remind myself that I'm speaking with real people, not just a mass of faceless humans. But that day, I couldn't seem to do it. I was just going through the motions. I couldn't get myself to relax.

My speech felt unnatural. It felt rehearsed. I wasn't relatable, because I wasn't sharing the real Jessica with my audience.

I was putting on a show.

And sure enough, after the speech was over, I saw the consequences of that. Usually, I make such a strong connection with the people I'm speaking to that they feel compelled to come up to me and share their own life experiences afterward. In a group of three hundred, at least twenty or thirty people will normally line up to talk to me. They look me in the eye and say, "Wow, what you said really resonated with my life. Thank you."

That day, only seven people approached me after my speech. And I knew I had missed an opportunity to connect with more people on a deeper level.

Later, I understood where I had gone wrong. I had neglected my physical balance before I took the stage. That resulted in a headache, which threw off my mental balance, which threw off my spiritual connection with my audience. Because I ignored my physical needs, the domino effect of imbalance kicked in and sabotaged my whole speech.

When one thing in your life feels out of balance, you have to address it right away. That's how you stop the domino effect of imbalance from taking over, and that's how you can consistently be your best self.

In Balance with One Another

The people around you, and specifically your significant other, can bring a big sense of balance to your life. Don't get me wrong: you don't need a significant other to have balance. But when you find the right person, he or she can bring even more balance to your life in new ways that you hadn't thought of before.

For a long time, I knew that something was out of balance for me. I felt as though there was always something missing. In part, that was because I didn't have a serious relationship for the first seven years of my speaking career. I dated on and off, but I didn't have a serious guy in my life.

That's when Patrick came along.

I met him in 2010 at a taekwondo school. I was preparing to do a demo at the World Championships, and I needed some private lessons from a taekwondo instructor. I decided to ask a friend of mine, Diana Perry—one of the head instructors at a school near my home—for some extra training.

So I showed up at this taekwondo school, and there was Patrick, a new teacher at the school. I didn't have any idea who he was. He was from California, and we'd never crossed paths. The only real connection we had at that moment was the fact that we were both in the same style of taekwondo, through the ATA.

Diana invited me to her house from time to time, to socialize outside of the school, and sometimes Patrick was there. So I got to meet him off the mat, and I got to know him as a person. We liked each other right away, but we had to keep it to a professional kind of relationship. You can't have a romantic relationship between an instructor and a student in a taekwondo school. It's frowned upon.

Then, finally, Patrick was invited to take over a taekwondo school in Phoenix. After he made the transfer to a different school, it broke our teacher–student status.

He didn't wait long to ask me out. In fact, he did it right after he finished his last official act as an instructor at our school in Tucson. The same moment after he locked up for the last time, he sent me a text message.

"Would you like to go to dinner?"

I was in Oshkosh, Wisconsin, in the middle of the largest air-show in the world, doing a series of speeches there. I still remember that moment because I heard the text message noise as I was about ready to go to bed. There was a two-hour time difference over there. I looked at my cell, and I saw his message.

It's about time, I thought.

"How Rude"

People often want to know exactly what Patrick's first reaction was to the fact that I didn't have arms. And I can tell them, because it happens that Patrick himself loves telling this story.

When I walked into the school that first day, looking for Diana, Patrick watched her go over to me with open arms to give me a hug. She hadn't seen me in years; we were all doing our own thing after college. Patrick saw her give me a hug, and he was really perplexed as to why I didn't return the hug. He assumed my arms were tucked in my sweatshirt, down at my sides.

So his first impression of me was, "How rude is that girl that she won't even pull her arms out of her sweatshirt and return this hug to her friend that she hasn't seen in years." Then his attention was pulled away by a student, and the class went on.

After I left, Diana explained to him how we had met, and why this random lady was showing up at the school. In the course of filling him in, she mentioned that I had been born without arms. "I helped her come up with a modified taekwondo form," she told him.

That was when Patrick realized that his first impression of me had been wrong. I wasn't being rude to my friend. I just didn't have arms.

He liked me better after that.

Authentic Balance

You know that you're in balance when things feel right naturally.

What I liked about Patrick from the beginning was that he was so transparent in the way that he reacted to things. He communicated. He talked to me like he knew me, and I felt naturally comfortable around him.

When people meet me for the first time, they often get hung up on the fact that I don't have arms. But sometimes I meet the rare person who sees past that kind of thing. That person just sees me for who I am.

Patrick was one of those people. To him, my armlessness wasn't a factor in who I was as a person. I loved that he could just see me for me, talk to me, and interact with me the way he would with anyone else. It's not every day that you run into someone without arms, so it's a natural thing for people to be surprised. But being able to see the real me was one of the special things about Patrick from the beginning. I felt from the start that he was very genuine.

We adapted to each other naturally. He's the kind of person who loves hugs, and I don't have arms. So I learned to hug him with my legs—"Jessica-style" hugs. In the car when we're driving, he holds my foot instead of holding my hand. It was never a big deal. We just work together that way.

We bring balance to each other every day. It's a balance of total acceptance, love, and security, but it's more than that, too. He likes how driven I am, and how persistent and adventurous I can be. He knows that when I set a goal, I will achieve it. He sees me as being fearless—and I bring all those things out in him. At the same time, he grounds me. When I'm ready to leap ahead without thinking, he brings in the common sense.

He is my ballast—the weight added to a plane specifically to bring its center of gravity to the right place. He is the weight of balance in the formula for flight of my life. Patrick isn't the kind of weight that drags me down. He is the weight I need to fly straight and level, always.

Balance in Flight

As the pilot in command of you, you have to keep the various forces around you in balance. Any one of those forces, left unchecked, can throw you off balance and cause your life to fall apart, much the way that if an airplane loses its balance in flight, it can start to fall from the sky. Everything going on with that airplane has to be in balance to allow it to fly.

If you're seeking balance in your own life, start by identifying what is most important to you. And when you find what is most important, make sure that is evenly taken care of so that you're able to get what you need from it. Understand what it takes for you to be healthy emotionally, spiritually, and physically. Then make those elements part of the way you live. Use them to lift you to success and propel you to your next horizon.

Just like a plane needs all the elements of the flight formula—lift and weight, thrust and drag—the needs of your life have to be in balance: your family, your love life, your career, and everything else that's important to you.

Perfect balance in all of these things gives you the optimal lift you need to reach the heights of your life. And once you're balanced, you have a strong foundation to disarm the limits on your flight path to success. The next chapter will take you through the power of persistence.

Speaking at the Pentagon in Washington, DC.

7

Persist against the Drag

When everything seems to be going against you, remember that the airplane takes off against the wind, not with it.

~HENRY FORD

Above All Odds

MOST PEOPLE ARE AMAZED by the actual physical act of me flying an airplane. But I think what they should really be most impressed with is the journey of learning to fly, because that was one of the biggest tests of persistence that I have ever known.

It started in October 2005, with my first flight lesson. I took that first step with Wright Flight, a nonprofit organization that uses aviation to help children achieve goals. They took me up in a Cessna airplane, the aircraft that most student pilots typically fly. But for me, that Cessna presented a host of logistical challenges. We realized quickly that flying this plane would require at least three if not four functional limbs. It just wasn't going to happen.

That was the first step on the long road to finding an airplane that would work for me. It took six months to find the next potential option—an Ercoupe I saw on the cover of *Aircraft Owners and Pilots Association* magazine. The Ercoupe got my attention because the article was about a kid with a disability who learned to fly the plane. He had a condition called spina bifida, which limited his use of his legs and spine. The same article described how the plane's owner, Glen Davis, had taught another man to fly the Ercoupe with only three functional limbs.

Wow, I thought, *this plane sounds perfect for me.*

The First Ercoupe

I immediately contacted Glen Davis, who invited me to Florida to start training. He volunteered to train me himself in his own airplane, at no cost to me. I was thrilled. This had to be the solution I was waiting for.

But after six days and thirty hours of intense flight training, it was clear that this airplane was not going to work after all. Glen decided we needed to find a sport-qualified Ercoupe airplane instead. Not only would it fit me better, but I wouldn't have to go through the medical exam that most pilots have to take before they can get their license. Sport pilot certificates are exempt from that. Which was good, because we figured that if anyone found out that a woman without arms was trying to fly, it would probably be an end to the whole dream.

Glen found a sport-qualified Ercoupe to continue our training in California. But after a few days, we were forced to admit that I couldn't handle the throttle. The throttle in an airplane is like the gas pedal in a car, but it's up high on the control panel instead of on the floor. It was too high for me to reach safely in case of an emergency. That was the end of any success in that plane.

By then it was February 2007. I'd gone through three airplanes, and I was stuck. I spent an entire year looking for another option without any luck.

I started to think, *Maybe I really won't be able to make this dream into a reality after all.* It was my lowest moment.

The Casa Grande Fly-In

But I wasn't ready to give up yet. About that time, another non-profit called Able Flight offered to help me with other options.

I looked up a picture of an Ercoupe airplane and made it the desktop background on my laptop. Every morning, I looked at that picture and envisioned myself flying that plane. I saw myself lifting into the sky, breaking through the clouds, and bringing my Ercoupe back down to earth for a clean landing.

Within weeks of putting up the picture, I found out that an antique airplane fly-in was coming to town.

The Ercoupe falls under the category of an antique airplane. So I got my family on board, and we went to the event. This was in the spring of 2008. I spent two days at the fly-in combing through airplanes, trying to find an Ercoupe that would be right for me. The only one I found wasn't in flying condition.

I headed back out to the parking lot with my parents on that second day, truly disappointed. I wasn't going to find my airplane after all. When we got to the car, we got our lunch out of the cooler, and my dad lit his pipe. I don't know many people who smoke pipes, but my dad is from the American South. Just envision an old southern man with a pipe in his mouth on a farm, and that's my dad.

At that moment, another man walked by who also had a pipe in his mouth.

"Hey!" my dad called out to him. "What type of tobacco are you smoking in that pipe?"

The man stopped, and we struck up a conversation. His name was Mark. My dad told him our story about how I was there hoping to find the right Ercoupe. "Oh, that so?" Mark said. "Well you know, my buddy Parrish Traweek over at the San Manuel Airport has an Ercoupe."

It was a sport airplane 415 model C Ercoupe without rudder pedals. Exactly the plane I needed.

"You've got to be kidding," I said. "What's this guy's number?"

"Actually, he's here at the fly-in," Mark told us.

We ran back in there to track down this Parrish Traweek, and that was my introduction to my third and final flight instructor. "I'll train you if you're at the airport tomorrow morning at seven o'clock," he said.

I made it to that seven o'clock meeting. Seven months later, I earned my wings.

The Power of Persistence

Everyone has come face to face with that moment when all you want to do is give up. When you experience that feeling, but find the will to push forward anyway, that is persistence.

Persistence connects to the "drag" element of the formula for flight, because overcoming drag takes great fortitude and drive. Drag is the resistance that an aircraft is up against as it pushes through the air—just like we sometimes face resistance or even failure on our journeys through life. When you have persistence, you have the drive to make it down the home stretch and make your dream come true.

Without persistence, you won't have what it takes to get where you need to be for takeoff. You won't have what it takes to keep moving forward when times get tough, when people doubt you, or when the world seems to work against you. But if you practice persistence, none of those things can stand between you and the success you desire.

The path to flight isn't always turbulence free. Obstacles will stand in your way, and you'll be tempted to give up. But if you have persistence, those obstacles won't stop you. In the end, they'll make you stronger.

Resist to Persist

Sometimes, doubt or resistance from the world around you can become your greatest fuel for persistence.

When I think back to what really drives me to get past that little extra hurdle, I think of a bully I met when I was in fifth grade. I was walking to the cafeteria, and a sixth grader came up to me with his arms in his shirt.

"Look, Jessica," he said, "I'm just like you. I'm handicapped."

At that very moment, the response to him that went off in my head was, *No, I'm not. I'm not handicapped.* Because my definition of "handicapped" at the time was that I couldn't do anything. *I'm not handicapped,* I stated to myself. *I can do things.*

That particular moment was the toughest experience I had in all my years of school. But do you know what? Every time I run into doubt in my life now, I remember that statement I made to myself, and it makes me stronger. "You can't drive without modifications," someone once told me. I learned to drive without modifications. "We've done everything we can to make you a pilot. I don't think there's anything left to try," someone else said. I became a pilot.

Every time I hit a rough patch, I remember that school bully. And it pushes me to a new level of persistence. It pushes me not to give up.

Speaking of Persistence

Persistence means adapting to the challenge in front of you, no matter how many tries or how much work that takes.

My speaking career is one example of this. When I started speaking in 2005, I thought, *Well, this should be easy. Speaking is going to be a grand old occupation.*

I found out fast that I had a lot to learn—even more so about the business end of things than about speaking itself! The part where I actually delivered the speech turned out to only be 10 percent of it. There were so many times when I struggled to get by financially. I had a second job as a secretary in a church. I even had to make DVDs using my own computer to sell at the back of the room after my speeches.

A few times, I had to take unpaid speaking opportunities. At first I didn't want to do that, because I thought I was going to lose credibility. But I finally realized that you have to start out that way.

Once I did a free speech for the Alzheimer's unit in a nursing home. Obviously, my audience wasn't really all there. After the speech, a lady came up to me and said, "Now see here, you can't go telling everyone that they should do anything they want. What if they want to jump off a cliff?"

No one ever had that kind of response to my speech. I just looked at that woman and said, "You've got a very good point."

Meanwhile, I persisted in learning the business behind being a speaker. Instead of one speaking engagement popping up here and another popping up there, I had to figure out how to get a continuous flow of them. I really didn't know what I was doing. My degree was in psychology with a minor in communication. But just about everything I've learned came by doing it: figuring out the pros and cons, and not giving up.

Speaking was no exception. Ten years after I started, my career was on solid ground. I had one full-time employee and a network of professional contractors filling in specific niches for me, like video editing.

And it wasn't all about the business end. Even with my speech itself, persistence paid off: each time I shared one of my stories on stage, it got better through practice. I have traveled to twenty different countries, and all that time, I shared those stories with others. I was helping shape the lives of people both with and without disabilities.

Know Your Guiding Star

For persistence to work, you have to know your motivation for why you do what you do. You have to know your guiding star.

Early in my speaking career, a woman confronted me about what I was doing. She felt as though people with disabilities who became motivational speakers were actually doing a disservice to other people with disabilities. Most disabled people were out doing ordinary things to make a difference in the regular world, she said. "They're teachers and carpenters. They don't run around everywhere trying to be in the spotlight."

That experience really made me question why I was speaking, and whether I was doing a service or a disservice to people with disabilities and to anyone in general. The more I thought about it, the more I remembered all the positive things my audiences told me about how the work I was doing changed their lives for the better. In speaking, I was making an impact on thousands more people than I could reach in a whole lifetime of doing an ordinary job. That's important if you want to make a change.

I got back in touch with my motivation for speaking. I realized that I might not be able to please everyone, but that was okay. It would be wrong to stop helping thousands of people for the sake of a few who disapproved. That would be the real disservice.

I continued speaking with more persistence than ever, because I felt confident that I was doing the right thing.

Persistence in Flight

Sometimes people say I'm stubborn. I say that stubbornness can work to your benefit when it comes to facing down a challenge. It gives you the grit you need to push through obstacles, disarm your limits, and take flight once you finally reach the end of the runway.

It gives you the drive to be the pilot in command of you.

Never give up on your goals. As long as you don't give up, you'll find yourself getting closer to achieving them. And on the way, you'll create a stronger foundation for your life.

But persistence isn't the only part of a strong life foundation. The people you surround yourself with also play a big role in your flight to success. Next, I'll show you how to identify and build a support system that will give you the lift you need to propel you to the next horizon.

"Create a life that feels good on the inside, not one that just looks good on the outside."

~ANONYMOUS

With Louisa during my trip to Ghana, Africa.

8

The Lift of Support

Be strong enough to stand alone,
smart enough to know when you need help,
and brave enough to ask for it.

~MARK AMEND

Louisa with No Arms

IN 2010, I WENT on my first speaking tour in Africa. I visited Kenya and then traveled to Ghana to speak to the communities there.

The last speech on my schedule was in Accra, the capital city of Ghana. We were in a huge auditorium in the center of the big city, so we were hoping that a lot of people would show up. Before the speech, I was in the green room going through my talking points when one of the organizers knocked on the door and led a woman in to meet me.

Her name was Louisa. She was probably about three feet tall, and she walked with a little bit of a limping gait. Her hair was short and straight. She was in her mid-thirties, with big eyes, ivory-colored drop earrings, and a yellow Sunday dress printed with flowers. But the most remarkable thing for me about Louisa was that she also didn't have arms.

She came up to me and said in fluent English, "I really wanted to meet you. I traveled from far away to be here today."

Then she told me her story.

Louisa had been born without arms—a congenital defect similar to my own. Unlike me, however, her disability was a stigma in her developing country. Her father left her mother, saying that Louisa was an animal and blaming her mother for giving birth to her. The rest of the community encouraged Louisa's mother to abandon her in the wilderness and let her die.

But Louisa's mother chose not to do that. She took Louisa away from the village and raised her in hiding. Louisa grew from a child into a capable adult. Finally, she came out of hiding and got a job as a first-grade teacher.

At first, the school community didn't know how to react to her. But she told me this, and I'll never forget it. "Because of my height, the children picked me as their favorite," she said. "They come to me to talk about their issues. They relate to me more than to the other teachers at the school." When she first began teaching, the school community thought her disability would scare the children. Instead, it had the opposite effect.

I saw the true passion in Louisa's eyes as she told her story. She was on a mission to make a change in the world, just as I was. She was making a difference in the lives of countless children. And that was possible because, early in her life, her mother chose to keep her instead of letting her die.

Everything Louisa does today is possible because of a single person who supported her when nobody else would.

Support for Your Dreams

Louisa's story inspired me beyond words. And she is just one example of the impact that support from others can have in our lives.

Support is part of the "lift" element in the formula for flight. Your support is the foundation you can always count on: the individuals who will always be there, even and especially when other people flake on you. Your support network is critical to your success. When you surround yourself with supportive people, they will help to get you through those tough days when life feels difficult to handle by yourself.

A strong support network will include people who are wiser than you and have more life experience, and you'll be able to lean on their greater knowledge when you face questions that your own limited life experience can't answer. Without that support network, you'll be misled, confused, and unfulfilled more than you need to be. You'll miss out on the rich development that you could have acquired from the older and wiser people around you, and it will take you longer to figure things out.

I went through a lot of negativity about not having arms when I was growing up. The people who supported me through those hard times lifted me out of my depression. They are individuals and groups that I cherish, because I realize that not everyone has that kind of support in their lives—like Louisa.

Support networks come in different forms, and we can't take them for granted. This chapter will take you through the various kinds of support that might be available in your life, and show you how you can return the favor by supporting others.

The Wind beneath My Ercoupe-Wings (Network of Support)

I may have been the first person to fly a plane without arms, but I didn't achieve that milestone on my own. I had the support of an incredible mentor: Parrish Traweek.

A lot of people I've met in my aviation career deserve credit in opening my eyes to the possibility of becoming a pilot. But Parrish was the one who really helped me follow through with that dream. He's a former Air Force pilot and mechanic, and he doesn't stand for having doubts. When I hit patches in my flight training that were physically difficult, he was always there to reassure me.

One of my biggest struggles was figuring out how to land. I doubted my capacity when it came to putting the plane delicately back on the ground. It really scared me. When that happened, Parrish had one thing to say: "You know what? You can do this." And he was right.

Parrish's reassurance was like a guarantee that my dream was going to happen, no matter what. That kind of support is priceless. You won't always be at the top of your game. As the pilot in command of you, there will be times when you're low on fuel. When that happens, you need a strong support network to help fuel you back up again.

Your support network can include family, friends, significant others, mentors, teachers, and even the larger community.

Family

For a lot of people, family is the first line of support. Mine is no exception. From the very beginning, my family was determined to make sure I would live a good life.

My mother poured her soul into giving me the opportunities to do everything I wanted to do. My father said he never once shed a tear about my birth condition—something that meant a lot to me, and still does. From the time I was little, he and I had therapeutic evening chats to help me get through some tough problems.

My siblings and extended family are also a huge part of my support network. Siblings are important, because they just believe in you by default. I have an older brother, Jason, and a younger sister, Jackie.

When we were growing up, they didn't treat me differently because I didn't have arms. They included me, fought with me, and played with me just like they did with each other. They believed that I could fend for myself and keep up with them, and they were right. Now, as adults, we are very close and we believe in each other to this day.

Extended family can also make a big difference in your life. Growing up, I had an aunt who was like a second mom for me. Her name was Cora, and I called her "Nanay," which means "mother" in Filipino. She was significantly older than my mother, and she had the dual role of a maternal aunt and a grandma. She strengthened my spirituality. So many people in my extended family strengthened parts of my life that I wouldn't have necessarily focused on otherwise.

Your family provides the support of truly caring about and wanting what's good for you, no matter what. Sometimes that's the greatest support of all.

Friends

A core group of friends can be another major part of your support network. I never had any issues making friends in school. When other kids tried to put me down because of my disability, my friends were there to pick me up.

My best friend was a girl named Stephanie. She and I never went to the same school, but we were the same age and we grew up together. We used to tell everyone that we were twins, because we looked alike and always tried to wear the same outfits. We went to the mall together, had sleepovers, and spent hours on the phone talking about our problems at school. Having that one best friend to confide in was a true blessing, because it gave me a sense of self-worth.

You can count on good friends to tell it to you like it is, in an unbiased way. Unconditional support is wonderful, but if you're doing something stupid, you need someone to tell you. That kind of honesty from true friends who don't hold back is an amazing form of support.

Significant Others

In my early twenties, my sister saw that I was struggling in the dating arena. So one night, she said a little prayer to God on my behalf. "God, please help Jessica find someone who can see her for who she is," she prayed.

Shortly thereafter, my husband, Patrick, appeared in my life. The kind of support he gives me as a significant other can't be described in writing. He motivates me, brings balance to my life, and inspires me to push my career and my dreams to new heights.

Your significant other is there to be a part of your life, through the tough times and the good ones. He or she shares your joys, tribulations, and triumphs. That kind of partnership is one of the most incredible and enjoyable forms of support you can have on your journey through life.

Mentors

The support of mentors and teachers can have a transformative effect on our lives.

One of my early mentors was Barbara "Barbie" Thomas. Barb is a beautiful bodybuilder who lost her arms in an electrical accident when she was a toddler. Before I met her, I had my doubts about things like marriage and motherhood—especially being a parent. Would I be able to handle children without arms? Change diapers? Pick them up and carry them around with me? I really didn't know.

Then when I was nineteen, my mom's friends called and said, "Tell Jessica to turn on channel 4. They're doing a special piece about this woman who is just like her." I turned on the TV and sat there in awe as I heard Barb's story. It wasn't the story of her not having arms that amazed me. It was the fact that she did everything just like me: with her feet.

Of course, I had to meet her, and she became a lifelong friend and mentor. When you find someone who can connect with your challenges on that kind of level, it's life changing. The first time I met her, I had three specific questions prepared. Number one: How do you take a jar down from a grocery store shelf with your foot? Number two: How do you push a shopping cart? And number three: How do you carry your baby boys?

She didn't just tell me the answers to my questions. She showed me. We went shopping, and I watched her take a big jar of pickles down from the shelf by clasping it between her toes and the arch of her foot. She showed me how she pushed a grocery cart by wrapping the bottom of her ribcage over the handle bar of the cart and leaning forward as she walked. Then, at her house, I saw her lift up her baby son using her chin and her shoulder to get a grip on his arm. It didn't hurt him at all.

People always told me, "Don't worry, you'll be fine. You'll be able to have children and do all that stuff." But Barbara's mentorship eliminated any doubts I had about whether I could really do what I wanted with my life.

"You can't let anyone keep doing these things for you," she told me. "Now that I've showed you how to do it, you need to go out and do this stuff on your own." She was that kind of support for me, and I cherish it to this day.

Find a mentor who pushes you to achieve your highest potential. Bring someone into your life whom you aspire to be like, and who will be your role model when things get hard. Give yourself the chance to benefit from that person's feedback and experiences. The support of a mentor will lift you up in ways you may not even have imagined.

Teachers

Like mentors, teachers can have a huge impact on our lives. They can help us better see what we can really accomplish. Sometimes they know us better than we know ourselves.

When I was in second grade, I wasn't behaving in class. It got to the point where I had to be reprimanded three times in one school day. Finally, my teacher, Mrs. Rossi, called my mom in for the dreaded parent–teacher conference.

We sat there as Mrs. Rossi told my mom about what was happening. Then she looked directly at me and said, "Jessica, I know you can do better."

The faith in those seven words transformed my academic career. When she said I could do better, I knew she was telling the truth. I went from an average student to a straight-A honor student for the rest of my schooling. That was the impact of one great teacher who believed in me.

Your teachers see the potential in you even when you can't see it in yourself yet. Listen to them, and try to see what they see.

Your Community

Sometimes support isn't just about the people you're close to. Support can be that person at the grocery store who smiles at you when no one else has that day. And sometimes support is the simple knowledge that you are part of a network that stretches around the world.

I am part of the global Filipino community. My mother is Filipino, and she made sure to instill in my siblings and me a connection to our cultural roots. Filipino culture values family, hard work, and persistence, and we were very much in touch with those principles when we were growing up. I made my first trip to the Philippines as an eight-year-old. We traveled back there every five years after that, and once I became an adult, I began to visit the country at least once a year. I consider that culture to be a huge part of who I am.

Today, my connection to that larger global community has made me a kind of ambassador of the Filipino-American community. People in the community know and support me, and I support them in return. Everyone knows me in the Philippines. I feel like a celebrity when I go there, because I can't go five feet without someone asking to take a photo with me.

Your community brings a sense of camaraderie, unity, and empowerment to your life. It reminds you to work toward the greater good—and the community will support you in return.

The No-Arms Club: Support Others

Just as the support of others lifts you up, the act of becoming support for someone else takes your life to new heights.

Supporting others is incredibly rewarding. I've mentored many girls without arms, and I love them to pieces. They are just like little sisters, and they look up to me in return.

One opportunity to support others came to me in July 2014. I was part of the committee that hosted the annual meeting for the International Child Amputee Network, which happened to be in Tucson that year. At the conference were four girls without arms. All of them were between four and twenty years old.

"Okay," I said, "this is going to be the No-Arms Club." The five of us piled into my Dodge Durango, and I drove them around town for the day. We went to lunch, we went shopping, and we bought ice cream. It was so special to have that kind of bond with these four other girls without arms—to see in their faces that I was making a positive difference in their lives.

Once you are in a position to lift someone else up, the reward for that support comes back to you tenfold. It brings true meaning and purpose to your life. The level of gratification is indescribable, knowing you made someone's life better—just by being you.

Find people to support in your life. You may not have to go far. Look for people around you who want to do the things that you love to do. Find common ground with people whose values are similar to yours, or whom you relate to well. If you live in an isolated area, you can even support others over the Internet.

Support can come to you in endless ways, and you can share it in countless ways, too.

Fire for Advocacy

When your support for others rises beyond the personal level, it becomes advocacy.

I have a fire for advocacy. Stories like the one about Louisa in Ghana remind me how important it is for me to do what I do as an international speaker. They ignite a passion in me to change the way people look at disability around the globe—to fight against the stigmas that still exist so that no child will ever be abandoned to die in the wilderness or be discriminated against by society.

Even in the United States, it wasn't long ago when children with disabilities were put into institutions instead of being allowed to attend normal schools. When I look at this history, I know that these things can change. It may take baby steps, but I will do whatever I can to change the unfortunate stigmas that exist today. My passion for advocacy has taken me on a whole new journey of support.

You don't have to march down the halls of Congress on Capitol Hill to be an advocate. Advocacy doesn't just happen on a large scale; it happens in everyday life as well. If you see any form of injustice, you don't have to stand by and do nothing. You can stand up and say something. Even if you think your act is small, your voice can make all the difference to someone who is suffering from injustice.

Support in Flight

Meeting Louisa in Ghana really hammered home for me the importance of support. She showed me the true value of having a support system, and it is a lesson I remember to this day.

Support is something we should never take for granted. You need to learn to acknowledge it, even when it appears in the smallest ways. If you don't acknowledge it, you can't recognize it. But if you're cognizant of the support you have, it will shift your attention from the negative to the positive. You'll be able to appreciate the people who want you to live a rich physical, emotional, and spiritual life. And that will help lift you up on your path to success—even on your lowest days.

It goes back to the formula of flight. Your support network is the lift you need to keep you airborne. Maintaining lift is a critical aspect of a pilot's job. You never want to be in a situation where you find yourself without lift, because that lift is what keeps you in the air. It gives you the altitude you need to disarm your limits and propel you to the next horizon—just like the supporters in your life lift you on your way to reach your goals.

Support from others will take you a long way. But there's one part of the formula for flight where you have to support yourself: authenticity. In the next chapter, I'll guide you through the power of self-honesty and show you how you can use it to take your life to the next level.

With my parents Bill and Inez, brother Jason, and sister Jackie.

9

Authentic Lift

No one can make you feel inferior without your permission.

~ELEANOR ROOSEVELT

Armed with Authenticity

MY BODY IS A form of authenticity.

When I was a little girl, I wore prosthetic arms to school compulsorily for eleven years. My parents, therapists, and medical specialists all had the best of intentions. They were trying to make my life better. They had no way of understanding that, for me, wearing those "fake arms" was torture.

I didn't take to them naturally, because I was born without arms. Imagine wearing an extra coat made of plaster with two extra limbs coming out of the shoulders. At the end of each limb is a hook. When you put on the plaster coat, it feels like wearing football equipment. On top of that, imagine you have olive skin, and the fake limbs are a very pale white. They don't match you at all; they just fill in the holes in your sleeves.

The worst part is that the limbs lack sensation. You can't feel whether something is hot or cold, smooth or rough. They're lifeless, and when you put them on, you feel less than human—as if you're half human, half robot.

That was how I felt. For those eleven years, whenever I wore my fake arms, I felt dehumanized. My first prosthetics were fitted at the age of three. When you're three, you are barely starting to develop your sense of identity and where you belong in the world. It made interacting with other children even more difficult, because being different is one thing, but being half-robot, half-flesh is really hard for children to grasp.

"What does it feel like?" they'd ask, coming up and touching the prosthetics on the playground. Or else they'd put their hands between the prosthetic hooks and tease, "Hey, Captain Hook! Are you gonna crush my hands?"

Every morning I'd put on the prosthetics, and I'd use them at school until the afternoon, when I was allowed to take them off. They frustrated me, because I could already do with my feet everything that these prosthetics could do. I could write faster, eat faster, grab things faster, scratch my head faster. The fake arms slowed everything down. I counted down the hours until I could use my feet again. When I finally got to visit the school nurse to take them off, it felt like I was a caged bird being freed.

Then, in 1997, my family moved from the small town of Sierra Vista to the big city of Tucson. And that opened the door for me to change everything.

I saw the move as a new opportunity to reinvent who I wanted to be to the rest of the world. We went from a population of thirty-three thousand people to a population of just under a million. None of these million people knew me yet. I was starting with a clean slate, and I knew it didn't include my fake arms.

So on the day before eighth grade started, I made a decision. I went through the usual morning routine; I brushed my teeth, combed my hair. I carefully picked out the clothes I wanted to wear to my first day at my new school. Then I went to find my mom.

She was in the family room, just passing through. My mom was always on the go. In this case, that worked for me.

"Mom," I told her, "I don't want to wear the prosthetic arms to school anymore."

My mom paused for a second and looked at me. "Okay," she agreed, "you're old enough now. It's up to you." Then she hurried off. And the same feeling of taking off the fake arms in the school nurse's office every afternoon flooded through me—like freeing a caged bird.

The next morning, I shaved my legs for the first time. I dressed in the clothes I'd picked out. I ate breakfast. I did every part of the usual get-ready program except for one thing: I didn't put on the prosthetic arms.

As I walked out the front door toward the bus stop, I knew my life had just taken a turn for the better. The hot, dry Arizona breeze touched my neck and back where the plaster of the prosthetics would have been. I had a sense of independence. I felt free. I felt proud. I felt sure of myself.

I felt honest about who I really was.

All the way to that bus stop, I couldn't stop smiling. *This is the day,* I thought. *Now it's time to live my life.* At the bus stop, another girl was already waiting. I could see in her face that she was nervous. Maybe it was her first day at a new school, too.

"Hi," I said. "I'm Jessica."

She looked up at me, and saw right past the fact that I didn't have any arms. "I'm Tamara," she said. "Hi."

That was how I met one of my best friends that year. Tamara and I sat next to each other on the bus and talked all the way to school. The two of us were good friends for the rest of eighth grade, and part of the reason for that is because it started from a place of truth.

It started with my authenticity.

Authentic Acceptance

Authenticity is being comfortable in your own skin. When you have the confidence to be your true self, you have authenticity.

A lot of us carry around "fake arms." Some of us even have a hard time letting go of them. But until you decide to make that move, you can never live an authentic life. And once you do take that step toward authenticity, you will feel so sure of who you are and what your place is in the world that people will notice from miles away.

True authenticity is part of the "lift" factor in the formula for taking flight. It will literally take your life up to the next level. And you will never go back.

Authenticity goes beyond the physical. You don't have to look far to see the different ways that people aren't authentic, and how that takes a negative toll on their lives. Some people do what's easy and predictable instead of pursuing what they love. Others feel as though they can't show their emotions. Sometimes people put on a persona to impress their peers so that they'll be accepted. They feel like they have to meet certain benchmarks to be "good enough," whether that means pressure from their parents or standards of success from society.

These all stem from the same fear: the fear of not being accepted.

If you can't accept yourself, you can't be authentic. True acceptance is freedom from the fear of rejection. It's the freedom to move forward with your life in the way that's best for you, without caring what others think. When you can accept yourself for who you are, you gain the kind of unfaltering confidence that gets you through criticism and the judgment of others.

Being who you are is risky. Sometimes there's a lot at stake. You might be in a situation where you worry that being who you are will put your job, your family, or your future in jeopardy. But in the end, you'll find that you're more resilient than you think.

You'll be proud that you got through that situation by staying true to yourself instead of putting on your "fake arms." And new opportunities will come to you that you never could have imagined.

Authenticity in Action: You Control You

When you're authentic, you draw a lot of positive people and things into your life. But almost as important, you learn to stay positive about yourself—even when others try to put you down. And that is a powerful tool for taking flight.

By not having arms, and not trying to hide it, I get all kinds of reactions from people. I've seen every response you can imagine, from both the positive and negative ends of the gamut.

Sometimes people are very blunt. They walk up to me and say, "My gosh, what happened to your arms? Were you born that way, or did you lose them?" Sometimes people react with pity. "I'm so sorry," they'll say.

In high school, a few kids made fun of me, pulling their arms into their shirts and saying, "Oh look, I am Jessica." Others responded with admiration. One day when my sister and I were at the mall, she overheard a guy say to his friend, "Did you see that girl over there? She doesn't have arms. Too bad, because she's pretty hot."

I've seen horror and fear. One time I was in Baskin-Robbins with my sister and I wanted to treat her to ice cream, so I pulled my credit card out of my purse with my foot and put it on the counter. A little girl was standing close by with her mother, and when she saw me put my foot on the counter she gasped and stepped backward, staring at me in shock.

Disgust is another reaction. Some people have OCD or just have a fear of feet. Once, I went to a bar in college to hear a band play. I showed up at the door, and the bouncer said, "ID?" I pulled it out from where I'd stashed it in my shoe and tried to hand it to him with my foot. He recoiled and said, "Oh no, I am not taking that. That's gross." He couldn't tell from what I was wearing that I didn't have arms, and he wouldn't let me in.

Curiosity is a pretty common reaction from kids. They'll come up to me wanting to see why I'm different, and I'm fine with that. Let the children ask questions; it will be a learning experience. It's the parents who rush over and grab them. They scold them and say, "Don't bother her," but curiosity really doesn't bother me at all.

In foreign countries, I've even seen stigmatization. On the same trip where I met Louisa in Ghana, I met with a provincial prince. He was honoring me for being in Ghana, and giving me a Ghanaian name, when a group of elders came by. One of the women in the group caught a glimpse of me, and the look of utter revulsion she gave me would have made most people feel like they weren't even worthy of being alive.

The worst part was, despite her obvious disgust, she couldn't take her eyes off me. She just stared and stared. That experience made me understand what it was really like to be someone with a disability in a developing nation, and it reaffirmed how important it was that I was doing what I was doing to increase awareness around the world for people with disabilities.

Probably the hardest reaction to deal with, though, is not being acknowledged at all. Sometimes people are so uncomfortable with my difference, they won't even acknowledge my presence. They'll look away, or if I'm with someone and ordering food, they'll turn to the other person and say, "What does she want?" as if I'm not a human. This happens all the time to people who have disabilities.

But in all honesty, the positive reactions I get from people far outweigh the negative. The majority of people have optimistic things to say during my encounters with them. I can't even count how many people have been positively touched by crossing paths with me. Sometimes, I even feel like it's more than just coincidence that certain people happen to meet me—almost like a little bit of inspiration and positive energy is what they needed that day, and God aligned our paths.

All of these reactions to authenticity—from fear to pity to curiosity—are inevitable when you are being authentic. They taught me that I can't control the way other people respond to me. I'm not here to make other people feel comfortable with my difference. That's their issue. My job is to live the life I have, and if people are uncomfortable, that's okay; let them be uncomfortable.

I have accepted that I will never be able to convince people to think one way or another. They have their own opinions, their own baggage, their own life experiences. So they can feel sorry for me if they want to.

What I can do is be confident in who I am. I have control of that. If I can't stop people from feeling sorry for me, they're just going to have to argue the point with me while I have a smile on my face. And if I'm the one making it through the hard days with the stronger positive outlook, then maybe the only ones they should feel sorry for are themselves.

My life isn't about convincing people not to feel sorry for me. It's about living out the joy in my many amazing experiences. That's the only thing that might show people that, "Yeah, I may not have arms.

But I'm living life. I have a wonderful life—a happy life. I've been given all this from God. And I'm just going to keep a smile on my face, because you never know who you're affecting."

That's how I respond to other people's reactions with authenticity. And when I do that, it puts everything in perspective. I understand that they're reacting the way they need to react, and that it doesn't have anything to do with the real me.

The only person who has anything to do with the real me is me. Once you realize that, you become a stronger person, and you empower yourself to take flight.

Authenticity in Flight

When I look at the career I've built as an international speaker, I see how much authenticity has had an impact on my life and the lives of those I meet. I didn't have to put myself out there. I could have played it safe. I had already accomplished much in my life, being a college grad and a pilot, among other things. But my mission was to take my message to the next level and use it to shape and strengthen the minds of others. My authenticity gave me the lift I needed to do that successfully.

That's why authenticity is such a critical part of the formula for taking flight. And that's why you need authenticity before you can truly become the pilot in command of you.

Today, I don't resent my parents or medical specialists for making me wear those fake arms. Despite my bitterness toward prosthetics, everyone had the best of intentions. It's very true that prosthetics do amazing things for people who were born with limbs, but then lost them in a tragic accident or a war, for example.

For me, those prosthetics had a different kind of benefit. They helped me define the line between who I was and who others thought I should be. And they gave me the challenge I needed to disarm my limits and push through adversity, into my authentic self.

Each of us faces the challenge of "fake arms" at some time in our lives. Each of us has the strength to overcome it through our authenticity.

The courage to be authentic is a huge and amazing thing. It doesn't come from nowhere. We find it in our belief in ourselves and, even more, in our belief in something bigger. The next chapter will take you through the final piece of my formula for flight in your life: faith.

My father, Bill, holding me as a newborn.

10

Faith: The Highest Lift of All

When once you have tasted flight,
you will forever walk the earth with your eyes turned skyward,
for there you have been,
and there you will always long to return.

~ANONYMOUS

Flying Solo

MY PATH TO BECOMING a pilot was a long journey that tested who I was at my core. It started with the adventure to go up in that single-engine airplane for the first time, and it tested my desire, courage, innovation, and persistence. It gave me a new appreciation for the balance and support systems in my life, and it pushed me to a new level of authenticity.

But my rise to being the pilot in command of my own success had one last surprise to offer me. And it appeared on the day of my first solo flight.

Your first solo flight as a pilot is like being dubbed as a knight or dame. It's the moment when your instructor has enough confidence in your skill level that he gives you permission to take off in his baby, his airplane, by yourself. "All right, you're ready," he says. "You can take the airplane up on your own now."

I trained for that moment over the course of three years, from Florida to Los Angeles to San Manuel, Arizona. I studied, practiced, and envisioned my desire to be a pilot.

The day my flight instructor, Parrish, finally told me I was ready, I was so excited that I couldn't even follow through with it. I invited all my friends and family to come out and watch, and I was so giddy that he finally came up to me and said, "There's no way I'm gonna let you solo this airplane right now. You're paying more attention to the people around you than to what you are doing. You're just too distracted; you're not on the ball."

I was crushed, but I couldn't argue with his judgment. He made that decision with my life, his airplane, and his job in mind. So we disbanded the party, and I went back to my hotel defeated. I came back the next morning still feeling low, ready to start back up with more training. I figured it would be a while before I got another chance at my solo flight.

I reached San Manuel-Ray Blair Airport at six o'clock in the morning on May 11, 2008—Mother's Day. I was prepared for the usual routine. Instead, Parrish turned to me and said, "If you can give me five good landings in a row, then I will let you solo this airplane."

Five Perfect Landings

It took a second for that to sink in. Around us, the morning was utterly clear and calm; there wasn't even a breath of air moving the windsock. The sky was cloudless, pale and cool; the air was fresh, and the sun was barely rising. There was only one other student pilot at the airport. "Okay," I said.

I gave him five perfect landings, and even I was in disbelief at how good they were. I was in the zone; my body was moving and fulfilling what needed to be done, but I almost felt like I wasn't connected to it. Like it was working on autopilot. I was fully present. I was in my element.

After the fifth good landing, Parrish said, "Okay, go ahead and taxi over there to the hangar." I knew that meant that he was going to be getting out of the airplane. A rush went through me. I was really going to do this on my own. I wouldn't have Parrish to lean on. I was going to be in the sky alone—with just my feet, the airplane, and God.

We did everything we needed to do. Parrish signed my logbook and put it in the Ercoupe with me, because that's one of the customary requirements for soloing. "Okay, now go ahead and taxi out, but check your radio before you take off," he said. The handheld radio would be my last link to him once I was in the air. "Make sure it works."

I taxied out and flipped the radio switch, just like he had asked. "Parrish, can you hear me?" I said.

"Loud and clear," his voice came back through the radio. "Go on down to the runway."

This is it, I realized. *Everything is squared away. I can hear him; he can hear me. I'm ready to go.*

I taxied down to the far end of the runway, inhaled a deep breath, and took off.

My Life in My Own Feet

The takeoff was beautiful. I was still in the zone, still in my element. The desert stretched away beneath me, all canyon and cactus, with an old mine off in the distance. It was breathtaking. As the plane rose into the air, I made my first turn, called a crosswind turn. And that was when I heard the static.

It was coming from the radio.

My stomach sank. *Oh no,* I thought, *don't tell me the radio is giving out.* I flipped the switch to talk, just like I had a minute before. "Parrish, are you there? I can't hear anything on the radio." No answer. All that came through was static.

That was the moment I realized that I was truly on my own.

I immediately snapped into my training mode. "Okay, Parrish is really not here," I told myself. "I can't communicate with him. He's probably panicking on the ground. What do I do? How do I handle this?"

And in my head, the answer came: *Fly the airplane first.*

It didn't matter that the radio was dead. It didn't matter what was happening on the ground. I had to fly the airplane first. Just like that, I tapped into my highest level of focus. All the hours of training were there to support me. I flew the airplane just as I had been taught. I went through every motion very consciously. My first approach for the landing was low and slow, so I throttled up and made another circle of the airport. I wasn't afraid to land. I just wanted to hit my landing perfectly.

And I did. The plane touched down so beautifully and smoothly that it left my other five landings in the dust.

Once the wheels were on the runway and I realized that I was safely in contact with the ground, relief swept over me, and I finally had time to smile. In fact, I couldn't stop smiling. When I taxied over to the hangar, Parrish was smiling too. As I opened the window to climb out, he came over to me. "Did I scare you?" I asked.

He didn't reply to that, but I could tell from the look in his eyes that he'd been nervous. He just wasn't going to admit it. "How was it?" he asked.

"Well," I admitted, "it was only the most incredible thing that I've ever done in my life."

It really was. That experience of launching into the sky, the radio not working, and the realization that I was really on my own with God brought home a powerful message for me. Nothing could have hammered it into my head the way that flying that airplane had at that moment.

I'd had my life in my own feet. And now, I also understood what was guiding them: faith.

Faith in Flight

My first solo flight was an incredibly empowering experience. It was the moment that asked me whether I was ready to pilot my own life. It made me fully realize for the first time that I am the one who alters the course of what happens to me. And my power to do that comes from faith.

Faith is an unexplainable reassurance that all things have a purpose and will come together for that greater purpose. When it comes to taking flight in your life, you can't do it alone. We all need faith to lift us up, especially during the most difficult and challenging parts of our lives. Without faith, you don't have the same sense of meaning and connection that you feel when you recognize that faith is on your side.

Faith is something you have to find on your own. My family is religious. We went to Catholic church every Sunday. I attended Sunday school. I came to faith through religion, but you don't have to have religion to find faith. My personal journey to faith unfolded with my life itself, through childhood, junior high, high school, college, and into adulthood.

My journey to faith was the most difficult journey of my life. It started with the question "Why me?" and ended with the belief that God has given me a true blessing by making me the way I am. I went through all five of the Kübler-Ross stages of grief—denial, anger, bargaining, depression, and acceptance—before I finally understood that the form God gave me is a gift.

Your path to faith may be a long one, too. But it will also be the most rewarding journey you'll ever take.

The Golden Egg

Faith doesn't need to be big and flashy. Sometimes it shows itself in small but powerful ways.

Growing up, I got a lot of these "faith clues." Between the ages of five and nineteen, when I was in that in-between phase, I started hearing from people—strangers who didn't even know me. They said little things like "Oh, you're so inspiring!" or "Wow, you are a blessing." When I danced as a little girl, people came up to me and said, "You have a lot of courage" and "God bless you." They were little things, little hints here and there—things that, looking back, could have been God speaking to me through many different people and experiences.

One of my favorite ones was the time I found the golden egg.

I was eight years old, and we were at an Easter egg hunt with my extended family. There were maybe twenty people there. At the egg hunt, every year, they hid one special egg. They wrapped it in gold aluminum foil and called it "the golden egg." If you found the golden egg, you won a special prize.

I desperately wanted to win that egg hunt. I wanted to prove myself. And I clearly remember looking up at the sky that day and saying, "God, if you just help me to find the golden egg, then I will be so faithful to you!"

Sure enough, I did find the golden egg.

That small experience was the beginning of a special bond between God and me. It started to open up my eyes to what "God" really means. Slowly, I started praying and opening up my communication with Him. I became aware of His responses to my prayers. That was my first real step on the path to faith.

As I grew up, I realized that "golden eggs" are everywhere in our lives. We just need to have the faith to pay attention, so that we notice when they're there.

Faith in the Plan

Sometimes the moment that we hit rock bottom is the moment when faith finds a window to shine through. A big part of faith is trusting in a larger plan, even when you can't see it.

When I was nineteen or twenty years old, I ran an errand that I'll never forget. I went to Sam's Club, a local warehouse store, and I was on my own. Before I even walked in, I was already having a bad day. I was grumpy. Nothing was going right.

This was right before the holidays, so Sam's Club was packed. Everyone and their mother was there, stocking up. There were lines and lines of people. And when I walked in, it felt like every single one of them turned to stare at me.

It was like a domino effect. As I walked by, heads turned my way, one after another. I was like the biggest magnet ever made, and their eyes were paperclips, just stuck to me. It was so overwhelming that I wanted to go hide behind a clothes rack. I felt completely ostracized.

Why, God? I thought bitterly. *Why can't I just be normal?*

Of course, God doesn't always answer right away. But a couple months later, I heard him loud and clear.

I was at the same Sam's Club, filling up my car in the gas station area and going about my business as usual. When I fill up my car with gas, I balance on my left foot and use my right one to hold the pump.

Well, a man came over to talk to me. He was with his daughter, parked in the car at the pump behind mine. And he said, "You know what? Can I just give you a hug?"

I looked at him, surprised. "Why?" I asked.

"You see my daughter over there?" he told me, nodding at his car where his daughter was. "She lost a couple of fingers not long ago. We've been so depressed about it. But when we saw you over here pumping gas into your car with your foot, she got over her self-pity."

After he walked away, I thought, *Wow! How rewarding is that to hear that I brought value to someone just by pumping fuel into my car?* Then I remembered my terrible experience at Sam's Club and how I had asked, "God, why can't I just be normal?" That day, I got my answer. "You're not normal, and this is why!"

When we feel like we're alone, faith reminds us that that isn't true at all. We're part of a greater purpose. In time, God shows us what that is.

A Foundation of Faith

Faith always surrounds us—even when we may not yet be ready to acknowledge that it's there.

My journey to faith took more than two decades. But even as I was walking that long road, the people around me had faith in me.

My mom had faith that I could have a normal, wonderful life. She gave me all the opportunities I needed to gain confidence. Her story is that, after I was born, she asked God why he made me the way he did, without arms. She just could not understand it. She could not see the light at the end of the tunnel. But it's true that you never know if God is working in mysterious ways. You just have to be patient and trust Him.

Twenty years later, my mom saw me on stage, sharing my message with thousands of other people. She saw for herself what an incredible difference I was making in those people's lives, as a result of my not having arms. And that was when she understood that God had a purpose all along.

I love my mom's story. But my dad tells one of my favorite stories of faith in my life that I've ever heard.

Not long after I was born, my dad was in the baby cry room, rocking me. He had just been through the experience of my birth, finding out I didn't have arms, trying to comfort my mom in the delivery room. The whole time, he never shed a tear. He was still cool and composed, but he was also pretty exhausted.

As he was standing there in the baby room with me, a woman came up to him. She realized that I didn't have arms, and that I was his daughter. And she looked right at him and said, "You know, you must be pretty special parents for God to bless you with a child like Jessica."

That moment pulled him through the chaos of everything that was going on. It was precious for me to hear, when I was growing up. That woman could have been an angel. She may have been God speaking through someone else. We'll never really know.

That's part of the beauty of faith.

Your Life in Flight

Straight and level flight is where you want to be, as a pilot. You have to take off, and at some point you also have to land. But while you're actually flying, straight and level flight is what you always try to maintain. Lift = weight, thrust = drag. These elements come into play to equal flight, just as adventure, desire, courage, innovation, balance, persistence, support, authenticity, and faith come together to help you soar to success.

That doesn't mean the skies will always be calm and clear. Life isn't always free of turbulence. There are times when we feel like we're helpless—like everything happening around us is out of our control.

But the reality is that we are the pilots in command of our own outcomes. We are responsible for disarming our own limits. We are responsible for what we do with our lives, and we can never use excuses from the circumstances of life to say we're not responsible for our actions. Even when turbulence happens, when radios break or shoes can't be tied, or even if we're born differently than the rest of the world, we still need to fly the airplane first.

We have to fly it the way we were born to, with authenticity. We need to take off with a thirst for adventure and a desire to succeed. We have to have the courage to face our fears and the persistence and innovation to pursue our dreams. We need to be willing to let the support of the people around us lift us to new heights, and we need to find balance in flight.

Most of all, we need to remember our faith. We may not be able to see the air or the wind beneath us, but that force is always under our wings. In that way, faith is our greatest blessing. It is the reason we can make the choice to fly.

Everyone has his or her own journey. You are already on yours. When you understand the power you have to give your life direction, and when you know that God is always by your side in the cockpit of your life, anything is possible. You can make it through the struggles and come away stronger than before. You can lift yourself to any level of success you desire, and you can propel yourself to the horizons you've always dreamed about. Most of all, you can have a profound, thrilling, and meaningful existence.

You are the one who makes your own choices. You are the one who determines what kind of life you will live.

You truly are the pilot in command of you. And that is the greatest gift of all.

About the Author

JESSICA COX IS THE first woman to fly a plane with her feet, a taekwondo black belt with a state champion title, a global advocate for disability rights, and an international motivational speaker who has shown thousands of people worldwide how they can live without limits.

Cox has riveted audiences in more than twenty countries and has spoken for leading Fortune 500 corporations, including State Farm, Boeing, JPMorgan Chase, and Oerlikon. Her message has also inspired millions of viewers on CNN, Ellen, and Fox. In 2012, Cox was named one of the 100 Most Influential Women by the Filipina Woman's Network, and she has also been recognized by the Inspiration Awards for Women as Most Aspirational in 2012 and Inspiration International in 2013, and by *Plane and Pilot* magazine as one of their Ten Best Pilots in 2013.

Born without arms, Cox broke through the perceived physical and mental limits of her birth condition to live an authentic and purposeful life. In addition to her 2011 Guinness World Record for being the first woman to use her feet to fly a plane and her 2014 State Champ title from the American Taekwondo Association, she has also surfed, skydived, paraglided, and earned her SCUBA certification.

But none of those accomplishments compare to her greatest triumph in life: her unrepentant regard and self-acceptance for herself, which gives her power and freedom far above any physical feat.

Cox's message of innovation, courage, and persistence in the face of setbacks shows audiences of all ages and backgrounds how to reach incredible heights of their own.

Cox lives in Tucson, Arizona with her husband, Patrick.

"Our deepest fear is not
that we are inadequate.
Our deepest fear is that we are
powerful beyond measure."

~MARIANNE WILLIAMSON

Become the Pilot in Command

Let Jessica Cox show you how to be the pilot in command of you.

As a motivational keynote speaker, Jessica Cox takes you and your team members on a journey of innovation, persistence, and ultimately triumph, helping you to "think outside the shoe" and turn the impossible into remarkable accomplishments.

Cox delivers her powerful and inspiring message through keynote speeches, seminars, online communities, and her documentary, *Right Footed*.

Inspirational Speeches

In her motivational speeches, Cox teaches audiences how to:

- ✓ Transform challenges into opportunities
- ✓ Redefine innovative thinking for incredible results
- ✓ Combine creativity, desire, persistence, and courage to achieve the impossible
- ✓ Reconnect with the power of their personal strengths and aptitudes

Cox's greatest triumph in life is her journey to faith. In her testimony speech, she encourages audiences to:

- ✓ Use life's trials to strengthen their faith
- ✓ Develop trust in God's plan and purpose in their lives
- ✓ Deepen their relationships with God through trust
- ✓ Renew their lives, spirits, purpose, and give glory to God!

Call or go online for Jessica Cox's speeches and talks.

Contact: www.jessicacox.com
+1 (520) 505-1359 admin@rightfooted.com

Seminars

Cox's "Think Outside the Shoe"® seminar helps audiences from all walks of life to tap into the powerhouse of their own ingenuity—and open the floodgates to new opportunities in their lives. Participants learn how to:

- ✓ Change the way you think about overcoming challenges
- ✓ Open your eyes to unexpected possibilities
- ✓ Use innovation to discover unexpected success
- ✓ Embrace resourcefulness to achieve limitless success

Call or go online to learn more about Jessica Cox's seminars.

Right Footed, the Documentary

Inspire yourself and your team with *Right Footed*, a documentary that opens a window onto the life journey of Jessica Cox. A story of resilience and hope that will touch anyone who feels different or limited and inspire them to look beyond their limitations, *Right Footed* invites you to walk with Jessica as she earns a college degree, two martial arts black belts, a driver's license, and her sport pilot's certification—all using her feet.

When Jessica's achievement as a pilot lands her in the Guinness Book of World Records, it launches her to a new level of prominence on the world stage. As her presence grows, Jessica emerges as a mentor to disabled children and an international disability advocate. Her personal transformation reveals the power of innovation and, ultimately, the limitless potential of the human spirit.

Right Footed is the story of one woman's courage, determination, love, and faith.

Call or go online to learn more about the documentary.

Facebook: www.facebook.com/JCMSofficial
Twitter: www.twitter.com/jess_feet

Photography Credits

COVER PHOTO:	David Sygall
COVER STOCK PHOTOS:	Shutterstock
INTRODUCTION:	Loida Duran Lansang in Linda Abrams' Ercoupe
CHAPTER 1:	Jessica Cox Motivational Services
CHAPTER 2:	Diveheart
CHAPTER 3:	Melissa Tan
CHAPTER 4:	Jessica Cox Motivational Services
CHAPTER 5:	Glen Davis in Linda Abrams' Ercoupe
CHAPTER 6:	Shanda Romans of ReiDiant Photography
CHAPTER 7:	Andrew McCabe
CHAPTER 8:	Patrick Chamberlain
CHAPTER 9:	John Braker
CHAPTER 10:	Jessica Cox Motivational Services
AUTHOR PHOTO:	Jessica Cox Motivational Services

www.jessicacox.com

Made in the USA
Middletown, DE
17 September 2024

60475763R00077